Transformational Thinking

TRANSFORMATIONAL THINKING

Harnessing the Power of the Mind

Dr David Kaluba

DK Global Publishing, UK

DK Global Publishing
Suite 1, 12 Cross Street
Wakefield WF1 3WE
United Kingdom

DK Global Publishing is part of the DK Global Group of companies based in the United Kingdom and Zambia

Published by DK Global Publishing
London, United Kingdom

ISBN: 9798335097444

©2024 DK Global Publishing (UK)
Published in the United Kingdom

DK Global Publishing is committed to a sustainable future for our business, our readers, our partners and our planet. This book is made from reusable sources.

Contents

	Acknowledgements	7
	Dedication	10
1	Introduction	12
2	Understanding Transformational Thinking	16
3	Foundations of Transformational Thinking	23
4	The Power of the Mind	27
5	The Mind's Limitless Potential	32
6	Awakening the Mind	40
7	The Power of Belief	45
8	The Art of Visualisation	53
9	Cultivating a Positive Mindset	61
10	The Power of Affirmations	67
11	Embracing the Journey	73
12	The Power of Neuroplasticity	77
13	Brain Physiology & Transformational Thinking	93
14	Building New Neuro Pathways	102
15	Techniques for strengthening Positive Neuro Pathways	108
16	The Role of Genetics & the Environment	115
17	Change your Destiny using your Mind	122
18	Cultivating Mindfulness	131
19	The Benefits of Mindful Practice	140
20	Developing Self-Awareness	146
21	Techniques for Enhancing Self-Awareness	151
22	Obstacles to Self-Understanding	157
23	Developing Emotion al Intelligence	161
24	Slip of the Tongue	172
25	Breaking Bad Habits	179
26	Strategies for Breaking Negative Patterns	185
27	How to Create New Positive Habits	195

28	Breaking Free from Addiction	207
29	Breaking Free from Phobias	221
30	Cognitive Behavioural Therapy (CBT)	229
31	Finding Meaning and Purpose	240
32	Support and Connection	249
33	Progress instead of Perfection	253
34	Overcoming Procrastination	261
35	Reframing Fear: From Threat to Opportunity	272
36	Mental Health Wellbeing	284
37	Success Through Transformation	291
38	Creating New Philosophies and Belief Systems	300
39	Constructing Empowering Beliefs	304
40	Living in Alignment with Personal Values	311
41	You are what you Think	320
42	Your Focus Determines your Actions	328
43	A Journey to Personal Fulfilment	333
44	Final Thoughts: Humans - An Indestructible Energy	341
45	About the Author	347
46	Epilogue	351

ACKNOWLEDGEMENTS

Acknowledgements

I am delighted to get this book into your hands, and more than anything, I am grateful for all your support and encouragement. I have no doubt, there will always be someone out there whom I will forget to mention here but please know that you are appreciated, and I thank you from the bottom of my heart for your tireless love and support always. To all my readers and those who support my work, I love you all and deeply appreciate you. Writing a book is not a solitary endeavour, and I am deeply grateful to my family and friends who have supported and inspired me along this transformative journey: your unwavering love, encouragement, and belief in me have been the driving force behind this book's creation.

To my family, thank you for your patience, understanding, and unconditional support throughout the ups and downs of the writing process. Your love has been my anchor, grounding me in moments of doubt and uncertainty, and your belief in my vision has fuelled my determination to see this project through to fruition. To my friends, thank you for your words of encouragement, your listening ears, and your invaluable feedback and insights. Your presence in my life has brought joy, laughter, and inspiration, and I am grateful for the camaraderie and solidarity we share on this journey of growth and discovery.

I am also indebted to the countless mentors, teachers, and guides who have shared their wisdom, knowledge, and expertise with me along the way. Your guidance and mentorship have been instrumental in shaping my understanding of transformational thinking and have inspired me to strive for excellence in every aspect of this book. Lastly, I extend my deepest gratitude to you, my readers who will embark on this journey with me. It is my sincere hope that the insights and wisdom shared in these pages will inspire and empower you to embrace transformational thinking in your own lives, unlocking your limitless potential and shaping a future filled with purpose, passion, and unlimited possibility.

With heartfelt gratitude,

David

DEDICATION

Dedication

To my dear friends and family,

This book is dedicated to you, my pillars of strength, my sources of love, and my greatest supporters. Your unwavering belief in me and your constant encouragement have been the driving force behind the creation of this book. To my three precious children, Joshua, Jacob, and Juliana, you are my greatest blessings and my most profound teachers. Your boundless curiosity, endless enthusiasm, and unconditional love inspire me every day to strive for greatness and to lead by example. May you always believe in the power of your dreams and the limitless potential within you.

To my dear friends, thank you for your laughter, your love, and your unwavering support throughout this journey. Your presence in my life has been a source of joy, comfort, and inspiration, and I am endlessly grateful for the memories we've shared and the adventures we've embarked on together. To my family, your love knows no bounds, and your faith in me has been my guiding light through the darkest of times. Thank you for your sacrifices, your wisdom, and your unwavering belief in my dreams. You are my rock, my haven, and my greatest source of strength. As I dedicate this book to you, my dear friends and family, I do so with a heart full of love and gratitude. May the words within these pages inspire and empower you to embrace transformational thinking and to live a life filled with purpose, passion, and possibility.

With all my love,
David.

1
Introduction

Welcome to "Transformational Thinking: Harnessing the Power of the Mind." In the pages of this book, we embark on an extraordinary journey of self-discovery, empowerment, and transformation. At its core, this book is a manifesto for those who dare to dream big, those who refuse to settle for mediocrity, and those who believe in the limitless potential of the human mind and the power that lies within. We are capable of so much more, and this book will get you started on a journey of self-discovery and personal growth. It will transform you from within in the most unique way possible, so sit back and enjoy the ride. Transformational Thinking is not just a philosophy; it is a way of life; it is a mindset that propels us towards greatness. It is about harnessing the power of our thoughts, beliefs, and intentions to create the life of our dreams. In this introductory section, we explore the essence of Transformational Thinking by dissecting its principles, in order to understand its transformative power.

The mind is the most potent tool at our disposal; it is a reservoir of untapped potential waiting to be unleashed. In this book, we look into the inner workings of the mind, exploring its extraordinary capabilities and uncovering the secrets to harnessing its power for success. From visualisation techniques to the power of affirmations, we unlock the keys to unlocking our mind's full potential. And before you finish reading this book, you will not only discover yourself but will learn practical tools to help you take your life to the next level of thinking and productivity. Success is not a destination; it is a journey: a journey of self-discovery, growth, and mastery.

As we journey together through the pages of Transformational Thinking, we explore the principles and practices that pave the way for success. From setting goals to overcoming obstacles, we learn how to cultivate a mindset of resilience, determination, and unwavering faith in our ability to achieve our greatest aspirations.

Transformational Thinking is more than just a means to an end; it is a philosophy of life and a way of being in the world. By the time you are done reading this book, you will hopefully embrace the transformative power of your journey, celebrating the victories, learning from the setbacks, and stepping into your fullest potential. With each page, you will move closer to realising your dreams, embodying your greatness, and inspiring others to do the same. After all, we are blessed to be a blessing to many. The human mind is an extraordinary tool, capable of shaping our reality, driving our actions, and determining our outcomes. In this chapter, we explore the immense potential of the mind and how harnessing its power can lead to profound personal transformation and success. Whether overcoming past mistakes, achieving personal goals, or creating a positive impact in the world, understanding and leveraging the power of the mind is crucial. It is probably the most important ingredient to achieving personal greatness, which transcends the ordinary and propels you to astronomical success. We will explore techniques and practices that will empower you to tap into your mental strength, including mindfulness, positive thinking, visualisation, and cognitive restructuring.

This book aims to equip you with the tools to unlock your mind's potential, enabling you to navigate life's challenges with confidence and purpose. By harnessing the power of the mind, you can transform your thoughts, actions, and ultimately, your life and destiny. I invite you to embark on this journey of self-discovery and transformation with me. The world belongs to the bold and courageous. Open your mind, expand your horizons, and dare to dream the impossible. For within you lies the power to achieve greatness beyond your wildest imagination. And whatever you do, dream big, as small dreams usually fade off when the going gets tough. Dream to the point where people start telling you that it is impossible, refuse to be average and mediocre. Allow your dream to push you to growth and ultimately, greatness. Welcome to the world of Transformational Thinking: where your mind is the paint brush that defines your world, where anything is possible, and success knows no bounds.

2

Understanding Transformational Thinking

Elements of Transformational Thinking

Transformational Thinking is the art of reimagining possibilities, transcending limitations, and embracing growth on a profound level. At its core, it embodies a shift in mindset, a departure from the status quo toward a reality where change is not only possible but inevitable. Transformational Thinking challenges us to break free from conventional thought patterns and established norms, empowering us to envision and create a future that surpasses our wildest dreams.

Reimagining Possibilities

Transformational Thinking begins with the ability to reimagine possibilities. It encourages us to think beyond the constraints of our current reality and explore what could be. This requires a blend of creativity, innovation, and visionary thinking, enabling us to see potential where others see limitations. By allowing ourselves to dream without boundaries, we open the door to a world of opportunities and solutions that were previously inconceivable, we effectively step into the realm of unlimited possibilities.

Transcending Limitations

Another fundamental aspect of Transformational Thinking is the transcendence of limitations. Often, our greatest obstacles are not external but internal, these are self-imposed barriers that stem from fear, doubt, or past experiences. Transformational Thinking involves recognising these mental constructs and developing the strategies and resilience needed to overcome them. It's about pushing beyond what we believe to be our limits and discovering the vast potential that lies within us.

Embracing Profound Growth
Transformational Thinking is deeply rooted in the pursuit of continuous growth and self-improvement. It invites us to view every challenge as an opportunity to learn and evolve. This growth mindset fosters a spirit of resilience and adaptability, essential qualities for navigating the ever-changing landscape of life. By embracing growth, we not only enhance our skills and knowledge but also cultivate a deeper understanding of ourselves and our capabilities.

Challenging Norms and Questioning Assumptions
At its heart, Transformational Thinking is about daring to challenge norms and question assumptions. It encourages us to critically examine the status quo and seek out new perspectives. This willingness to question and innovate is the driving force behind societal progress and personal transformation. It empowers us to break free from limiting beliefs and adopt a more expansive and inclusive worldview.

Envisioning an Extraordinary Future
Finally, Transformational Thinking is about envisioning a future that surpasses our wildest dreams. It inspires us to set audacious goals and strive for extraordinary achievements. By cultivating a bold and optimistic outlook, we can

manifest a reality that aligns with our highest aspirations and values. This forward-thinking approach not only fuels personal success but also contributes to the collective advancement of society. In essence, Transformational Thinking is a powerful framework that redefines what is possible. It challenges us to transcend our limitations, embrace continuous growth, and envision a future brimming with potential. By adopting this mindset, we empower ourselves to create meaningful change and achieve a higher level of personal and collective fulfilment

Importance of Mindset and Personal Growth
Mindset is the lens through which we perceive the world, a filter that shapes our thoughts, beliefs, and actions. In the realm of Transformational Thinking, mindset is everything. It's the difference between stagnation and growth, between limitation and possibility. By cultivating a mindset of curiosity, resilience, and openness to change, we unlock the door to personal growth and self-actualisation.

Components of a Transformative Mindset

1. **Curiosity:**
- Cultivating an eagerness to learn and explore.
- Seeking deeper understanding by keeping an open mind and asking questions.
- Embracing the unknown as a pathway to discovery.

2. **Resilience:**

- Developing the strength to bounce back from setbacks.
- Viewing failures as learning experiences.
- Maintaining a positive outlook despite challenges.

3. **Openness to Change:**
- Being flexible and adaptable in the face of new circumstances.
- Letting go of rigid beliefs and being willing to shift perspectives.
- Embracing new ideas and approaches.

Neuroplasticity and Transformational Thinking

Neuroplasticity is the brain's remarkable capacity to reorganise itself in response to new experiences, learning, and environmental influences. It's the biological foundation of Transformational Thinking, the mechanism through which we reshape our neural pathways and rewire our minds for growth and transformation. By understanding the role of neuroplasticity in shaping our thoughts, behaviours, and emotions, we gain insight into the profound potential of the human brain to adapt, evolve, and thrive. The science world now understands that our brains have the ability to change and adapt as required.

The Journey Ahead

In the chapters that follow, we will look deeper into each aspect of Transformational Thinking. We will explore practical strategies, exercises, and insights to cultivate a mindset of possibility, navigate change with grace, and unleash the boundless potential within us. This transformative journey will guide us in unlocking the power of our minds and embracing a life of limitless possibility. Here are some key aspects of Neuroplasticity that we will explore in the next few chapters to provide better understanding and clarity:

1. **Brain Reorganisation:**
   - How the brain forms new neural connections.
   - The impact of learning and experience on brain structure.
   - The brain's ability to compensate for injuries and adapt to new situations.

2. **Influence of Learning and Environment:**
   - The role of continuous learning in maintaining cognitive flexibility.
   - How environmental factors can stimulate brain development.
   - The importance of mental and physical activities in promoting neuroplasticity.

3. **Reshaping Neural Pathways:**
   - Techniques to consciously influence brain reorganisation through deliberate action.
   - The significance of repetitive practice and mindfulness.
   - How positive and negative experiences can alter neural circuits.

4. **Mindfulness and Meditation:**
   - Practices to enhance awareness and presence.
   - Techniques for focusing the mind and reducing stress.
   - Benefits of mindfulness for neuroplasticity and mental well-being.

5. **Goal Setting and Visualisation:**
   - Methods for setting realistic and inspiring goals.
   - Harnessing the power of visualisation.
   - Steps to create a clear vision for the future.

6. **Reflective Journaling:**
   - The importance of self-reflection in personal growth.
   - Prompts and exercises for deeper introspection.
   - How journaling can reveal patterns and insights for growth.

7. **Learning and Continuous Improvement:**
   - Embracing a lifelong learning mindset.
   - Strategies for acquiring new skills and bridging knowledge gaps.
   - The impact of continuous learning on brain health.

Join me on this transformative journey as we embark on a quest to unlock the power of our minds and embrace a life of limitless possibility. Together, we will explore the depths of Transformational Thinking and discover the extraordinary unlimited potential that lies within each of us.

3

Foundations of Transformational Thinking

Paradigm Shifts: Embracing New Perspectives

In the tapestry of our lives, there come moments when the fabric of our reality is stretched, challenged, and ultimately transformed. These are the moments of paradigm shifts; profound shifts in our beliefs, perspectives, and understanding of the world around us. In this chapter, we look into the transformative power of paradigm shifts, exploring their significance, their catalysts, and their role in our journey towards personal growth and enlightenment.

The Nature of Paradigms:
Paradigms are the lenses through which we perceive reality – the filters that shape our thoughts, beliefs, and actions. They are the invisible frameworks that govern our lives, dictating what is possible and what is not. To embrace new perspectives, we must first recognise the limitations of our current paradigms and acknowledge the need for change.

The Catalyst for Transformation:
Paradigm shifts often arise in moments of crisis, challenge, or disruption – moments when the status quo is no longer tenable, and the call for change becomes deafening. Whether it be a personal crisis, a global pandemic, or a technological revolution, these catalysts serve as wake-up calls, nudging us out of our comfort zones and into the realm of possibility. Until you become uncomfortable in your current situation, you will not make a move for a better life. The comfort zone is not your friend.

Techniques for Shifting Paradigms

Questioning Assumptions: Paradigms are built on a foundation of assumptions – beliefs that are often taken for granted and rarely questioned. To shift paradigms, we must become detectives of our own minds, interrogating our beliefs, and challenging our assumptions. By asking probing questions and seeking alternative perspectives, we open the door to new possibilities and expand our mental horizons.

Cultivating Curiosity: Curiosity is the fuel that drives paradigm shifts – the insatiable thirst for knowledge, understanding, and growth. By cultivating curiosity, we become explorers of the unknown, adventurers of the mind, and pioneers of new frontiers. With each question asked, each idea explored, and each perspective considered, we inch closer to enlightenment and transformation.

Practicing Empathy: Empathy is the bridge that connects us to others – the ability to see the world through their eyes, feel their emotions, and understand their perspectives. By practicing empathy, we break down the barriers that divide us, dissolve the prejudices that separate us, and cultivate a sense of connection and unity with all beings.

A Case for Successful Paradigm Shifts

1. **Scientific Revolutions:** Throughout history, scientific revolutions have reshaped our understanding of the cosmos, from the Copernican revolution that dethroned

Earth from its position at the centre of the universe to the quantum revolution that revealed the bizarre and counterintuitive nature of reality. These paradigm shifts not only transformed our understanding of the world but also revolutionised the way we live, work, and interact with each other.

2. **Social Movements:** Social movements have the power to ignite paradigm shifts on a global scale, challenging deeply entrenched beliefs and catalysing profound social change. From the civil rights movement that challenged racial segregation to the fight for human rights in society and political movements around the world.

Paradigm shifts are the engines of progress, the catalysts of change, and the harbingers of transformation. They remind us that reality is not fixed but fluid, that truth is not absolute but evolving, and that growth is not optional but inevitable. So, dare to question, dare to explore, and dare to shift your paradigm, for within you lies the power to transform your reality and create a future of limitless potential.

4

The Power of the Mind

The Power of the Mind

In the vast expanse of the universe, there exists a power so extraordinary, yet often overlooked – the power of the human mind. Within each of us lies a reservoir of untapped potential, waiting to be discovered, explored, and harnessed for transformative change. In this chapter, we look into the depths of our consciousness, unlocking the secrets of the mind and unleashing its boundless power to manifest our dreams and shape our reality. The power of the mind is an unparalleled force, wielding the ability to shape our reality, dictate our perceptions, and manifest our destiny. Within the intricate networks of neurons and synapses lies a reservoir of potential waiting to be unleashed.

It is through the mind that we navigate the complexities of existence, transforming thoughts into actions, dreams into realities. From the depths of despair to the heights of triumph, the mind serves as both architect and sculptor of our experiences, moulding our perceptions, beliefs, and attitudes in profound ways. With focused intention and unwavering determination, the mind has the capacity to overcome obstacles, transcend limitations, and unlock the doors to boundless potential. Truly, the power of the mind is a remarkable gift, offering us the keys to unlock the vast treasures of our innermost selves and forge a path towards personal growth, fulfilment, and enlightenment.

The power of the mind is a profound and multifaceted phenomenon that transcends the boundaries of physical reality, shaping our perceptions, experiences, and ultimately, our lives. At its core, the power of the mind encompasses the complex interplay of thoughts, beliefs, emotions, intentions, and subconscious processes that influence our behaviour, decisions, and outcomes. Here are some key aspects of the power of the mind:

Conscious and Subconscious Influence
The mind operates on both conscious and subconscious levels, each exerting its own unique influence on our thoughts, behaviours, and perceptions of reality. While conscious thoughts and intentions are within our awareness and control, the subconscious mind operates beneath the surface, shaping our beliefs, habits, and automatic responses based on past experiences, conditioning, and internalised beliefs.

The Subconscious Mind
Beneath the surface of our conscious awareness lies the vast expanse of the subconscious mind – a repository of memories, beliefs, and programming that shapes our perceptions and behaviours. By harnessing the power of the subconscious through techniques such as visualisation, and affirmation, we bypass the limitations of the conscious mind and tap into the limitless potential of our subconscious mind.

Creative Visualisation and Manifestation

One of the most potent expressions of the power of the mind is creative visualisation – the process of mentally picturing desired outcomes and experiences with clarity, detail, and emotional intensity. Through visualisation, we harness the creative power of our minds to align our thoughts and emotions with our goals, thereby influencing the circumstances and opportunities that manifest in our lives.

Belief and Expectation

Belief is a powerful force that shapes our reality, influencing our perceptions, decisions, and actions. When we believe in our abilities, possibilities, and the inherent goodness of life, we open ourselves to a world of opportunities and experiences. Conversely, limiting beliefs and negative expectations can create self-imposed barriers that hinder our growth and progress.

Mind-Body Connection

The mind-body connection highlights the intricate relationship between mental and physical health, demonstrating how thoughts and emotions can profoundly impact physiological processes and overall well-being. Positive thoughts and emotions have been linked to improved immune function, cardiovascular health, and longevity, while chronic stress, negativity, and unresolved emotional trauma can and does often contribute to a range of physical and mental health issues.

Self-Healing and Transformation

The power of the mind extends to the realm of self-healing and transformation, as evidenced by the placebo effect, spontaneous remissions, and the remarkable resilience of the human spirit in overcoming adversity. Through practices such as mindfulness, meditation, and hypnosis, individuals can tap into their innate capacity for self-regulation, resilience, and inner healing, catalysing profound shifts in perception, behaviour, and well-being.

Influence on Reality and Perception

Our perceptions shape our reality, and the power of the mind influences how we interpret and respond to the world around us. Cultivating a mindset of optimism, gratitude, and possibility, transforms even the most challenging circumstances into opportunities for growth, learning, and empowerment. Through the lens of the mind, we perceive not only the external world but also the infinite potential within ourselves. In essence, the power of the mind is a limitless force that resides within each of us, waiting to be harnessed.

5

The Mind's Limitless Potential

Understanding the Mind's Limitless Potential

The Mind-Body Connection: The mind and body are not separate entities but interconnected aspects of our being, each influencing and shaping the other in profound ways. By understanding the intricate relationship between our thoughts, emotions, and physical health, we unlock the key to holistic well-being and unleash the power of the mind to heal, rejuvenate, and thrive.

The human mind is a boundless reservoir of potential, a vast expanse of untapped possibilities waiting to be explored and harnessed. Within its depths lie the seeds of creativity, innovation, and transformation, capable of transcending the constraints of reality and manifesting the extraordinary. From the depths of our imagination spring forth worlds yet to be discovered, ideas yet to be conceived, and solutions yet to be realised. The limitless potential of the human mind knows no bounds, reaching beyond the confines of space and time to shape the course of history and redefine the very fabric of existence. It is a source of light in the darkness, a guiding force that propels us towards greatness and empowers us to create a future of infinite possibility and boundless potential.

The Creative Force Within
The mind is a creative powerhouse; a generator of ideas, inspirations, and innovations that have shaped the course of human history. From the works of art that adorn our museums to the technological marvels that define our modern age, the

power of the human mind to imagine, create, and manifest the seemingly impossible knows no bounds.

Awakening the Dormant Forces

The Power of Intention
Intention is the seed from which all manifestations grow – the guiding force that directs the energy of the mind towards a specific outcome. By setting clear intentions and aligning our thoughts, beliefs, and actions with our deepest desires, we activate the dormant forces within us and unleash the power of manifestation to bring our dreams to life.

Mastery Through Mindfulness and Presence
Mindfulness is the practice of being fully present in the moment, without judgment or attachment to the past or future. By cultivating mindfulness through practices such as meditation, breathwork, and mindfulness-based stress reduction, we quiet the chatter of the mind, deepen our connection to the present moment, and access the profound wisdom and clarity that reside within us.

Emotional Intelligence
Emotional intelligence is the ability to recognise, understand, and manage our emotions, as well as the emotions of others. By developing emotional intelligence through practices such as self-awareness, empathy, and emotional regulation, we harness the power of our emotions as a source of insight, motivation, and connection, rather than a source of confusion,

conflict, and suffering. We will discuss emotional intelligence in more detail in a separate chapter to give better and clearer understanding.

Understanding the unlimited potential of the human mind unveils a journey of discovery and empowerment, revealing the boundless capabilities that lie within everyone. At its core, this understanding transcends conventional limitations, acknowledging the profound capacity of the mind to shape reality, expand consciousness, and catalyse transformative change. Here are some key insights into the unlimited potential of the human mind:

Infinite Creativity and Innovation
The human mind is a wellspring of creativity and innovation, capable of generating novel ideas, solutions, and artistic expressions that transcend conventional boundaries. From scientific breakthroughs to works of art, the mind's ability to imagine, conceptualise, and manifest new possibilities knows no limits, fostering progress and evolution across all domains of human endeavour. The mind is quite literally an unlimited resource for every success you can ever imagine.

Adaptive Learning and Growth
One of the most remarkable aspects of the human mind is its capacity for adaptive learning and growth. Through experiences, exploration, and reflection, you can continuously expand your knowledge, skills, and perspectives, transcending previous limitations and evolving

into an ever more complex and capable person. This inherent plasticity allows for lifelong learning and personal development, enabling you to thrive in a dynamic and ever-changing world.

Healing and Self-Regulation
The human mind possesses inherent mechanisms for healing, self-regulation, and resilience, tapping into the body's innate capacity for health and well-being. Through practices such as mindfulness, meditation, and positive visualisation, you can harness the mind's power to promote physical, emotional, and spiritual healing, facilitating profound transformations and holistic wellness.

Conscious Evolution and Self-Actualisation
At its highest potential, the human mind serves as a catalyst for conscious evolution and self-actualisation, guiding you towards the realisation of your deepest aspirations and highest potential. By aligning with your inner truth, purpose, and values, you can unlock the latent capacities of your mind, transcending limiting beliefs and societal conditioning to embody a life of authenticity, and meaningful contribution.

Connection to Universal Consciousness
Beyond individual capabilities, the human mind is intrinsically connected to the vast expanse of universal consciousness, tapping into a collective reservoir of wisdom, insight, and intuition. Through practices such as meditation, contemplation, and spiritual inquiry, you can access higher

states of awareness and insight, transcending the limitations of the egoic mind and aligning with the universal flow of life. Everything is interconnected in the universe, every object serves as a link in a never-ending and unbreakable chain, forming the universal character. You are undoubtedly an integral part to this chain.

Co-Creation with the Universe

Recognising your inherent interconnectedness with the universe helps you harness the power of the mind to co-create your reality in alignment with your highest intentions and values. Through conscious intention, visualisation, and manifestation practices, you can collaborate with the creative forces of the universe to manifest your dreams, desires, and aspirations, unlocking the limitless potential of your mind to shape your destiny. In essence, understanding the unlimited potential of the human mind is an invitation to explore the depths of consciousness, unlock hidden potentials, and embark on a journey of self-discovery, growth, and transformation. By embracing the inherent creativity, adaptability, and resilience of the mind, you can transcend limitations, actualise your fullest potential, and contribute to the collective evolution of humanity and the cosmos. In the crucible of the mind, we discover the power to transcend our limitations, overcome our fears, and manifest our dreams.

6

Awakening the Mind

Awakening the Mind

Awakening the mind is a transformative journey of self-discovery and empowerment. It involves unveiling the layers of conditioning and limitations that veil our true essence. This journey begins with the realisation that within each of us lies the power to shape our destiny, transcend the constraints of the past, and embrace the boundless potential of the present moment. Through mindfulness practices, introspection, and self-reflection, we peel back the layers of unconscious programming and societal conditioning, allowing our true nature to shine forth. As we develop awareness and presence, we awaken to the interconnectedness of all beings and the inherent wisdom within us. Each breath and moment of stillness brings us closer to inner exploration, uncovering the depths of our being and embracing infinite possibilities.

Key Insights into Awakening the Mind

1. Cultivating Awareness and Presence

At the heart of awakening the mind lies the practice of cultivating awareness and presence in the present moment. By becoming fully present to our thoughts, emotions, and sensations without judgment or attachment, we awaken to the richness and depth of our inner experience, gaining insight into the nature of our minds and the patterns that shape us.

Table: Benefits of Cultivating Awareness

Benefit	Description
Increased Insight	Gaining understanding of personal patterns
Emotional Regulation	Managing emotions more effectively
Enhanced Well-being	Improving overall mental and emotional health
Greater Presence	Being fully engaged in the current moment

2. Questioning Assumptions and Beliefs

Awakening the mind involves questioning the assumptions, beliefs, and narratives that have been inherited or imposed upon us by society, culture, and past conditioning. Through introspection and inquiry, we challenge the validity of these beliefs, opening ourselves to new perspectives, possibilities, and ways of being in the world.

Graph: Process of Questioning Beliefs

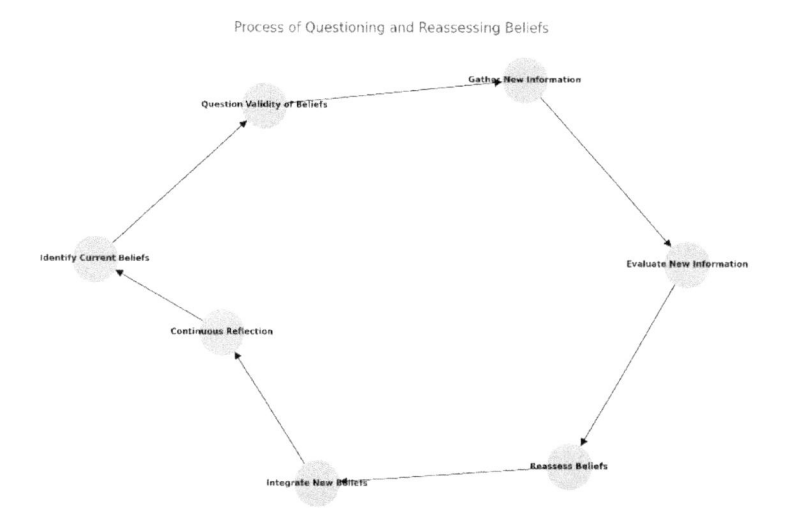

Figure 1: Graph illustrating the process of questioning and reassessing beliefs.

This visual representation shows the cyclical nature of evaluating and updating beliefs through continuous reflection. The steps for questioning beliefs include:

- Identify Current Beliefs
- Question Validity of Beliefs
- Gather New Information
- Evaluate New Information
- Reassess Beliefs
- Integrate New Beliefs
- Continuous Reflection (leading back to identifying current beliefs)

This iterative process helps in fostering a mindset of continuous learning and adaptability.

3. Embracing Uncertainty and Impermanence
The process of awakening invites us to embrace the inherent uncertainty and impermanence of life. Recognising that change is inevitable, we learn that clinging to fixed notions of identity or reality leads to suffering. By surrendering to the flow of life and embracing the unknown, we cultivate resilience, adaptability, and freedom from attachment.

4. Cultivating Curiosity and Wonder
Awakening the mind involves cultivating a spirit of curiosity, wonder, and openness to the mysteries of existence. By approaching life with a beginner's mind, free from preconceived notions or expectations, we open ourselves to the beauty, complexity, and interconnectedness of all phenomena, experiencing each moment with fresh awe.

Table: Attributes of a Beginner's Mind

Attribute	Description
Curiosity	Eagerness to explore and learn
Openness	Willingness to accept new experiences and ideas
Wonder	Appreciation for the beauty and mystery of life
Non-judgment	Observing without preconceived notions

5. Intuition and Inner Guidance

As we awaken the mind, we learn to honour and trust our intuition, inner wisdom, and guidance. Recognising that true knowledge arises from a deeper place within ourselves, we quiet the noise of the external world and attune to the subtle whispers of our inner voice. This practice provides clarity, insight, and direction on our path of self-discovery and growth. This intuition is sometimes referred to as your '6th sense' or in more common terms, your 'gut feeling', and if you connect with it, it might save you a whole lot of trouble.

Graph: Inner Guidance and Decision-Making

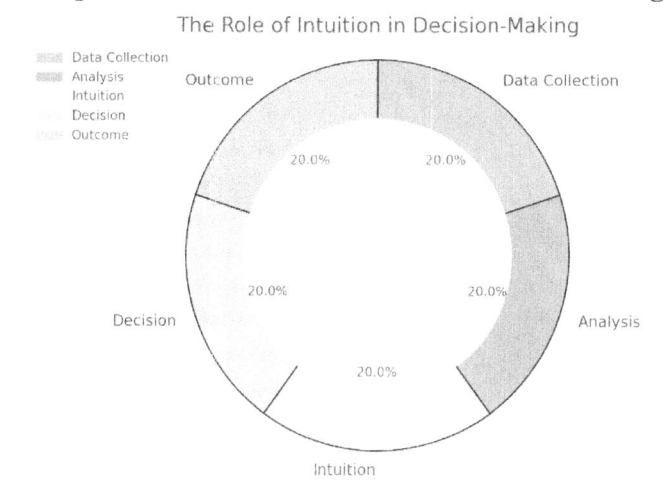

Figure 1: Graph illustrating the role of intuition in decision-making. Each section represents a step in the decision-making process, with intuition being one of the key components.

6. The Journey of Self-Discovery

Awakening the mind is not a destination but a continual journey of self-discovery, growth, and evolution. It requires courage, humility, and a willingness to confront the shadows and uncertainties that lie within us. Awakening the mind is a sacred and transformative process that invites us to transcend the limitations of egoic consciousness and align with the deeper truths of our existence. It is a journey of awakening to our true nature as spiritual beings, interconnected with all of creation, and empowered to co-create a reality of love, wisdom, and compassion.

7

The Power of Belief

The Power of Belief

The power of belief is a transformative force that shapes our reality and dictates the course of our lives. It is through our beliefs that we construct the lens through which we perceive the world, influencing our thoughts, emotions, and actions. Whether positive or negative, our beliefs have the remarkable ability to manifest themselves in our experiences, shaping the outcomes we encounter and the opportunities we attract. With unwavering conviction and faith, belief has the power to move mountains, overcome obstacles, and unlock the door to boundless potential. It is the fuel that ignites our passions, propels us towards our goals, and empowers us to create the life we desire. We get to tap into an infinite wellspring of strength, resilience, and determination, propelling us towards greatness and fulfilling our aspirations.

The power of belief is a fundamental force that shapes our perceptions, experiences, and ultimately, our reality. Beliefs are the lenses through which we interpret the world, influencing our thoughts, emotions, and actions in profound ways. Whether conscious or subconscious, positive or negative, our beliefs have the power to create or constrain our potential, shaping the course of our lives. Here are some key insights into the power of belief:

Key Insights into the Power of Belief

Influence on Perception and Interpretation
Beliefs serve as filters through which we interpret our experiences and make sense of the world around us. They shape our perceptions, colouring our thoughts, emotions, and behaviours, and influencing how we respond to various situations and stimuli. For example, someone who believes in their own abilities and worthiness is more likely to approach challenges with confidence and resilience, while someone who harbours self-doubt or limiting beliefs may perceive obstacles as insurmountable barriers.

Table: Positive vs. Negative Beliefs

Positive Beliefs	Negative Beliefs
"I can achieve my goals."	"I am not capable enough."
"Challenges help me grow."	"Challenges are insurmountable."
"I am worthy of success."	"Success is out of reach for me."

Impact on Behaviour and Choices
Beliefs have a direct impact on our behaviour and decision-making processes, guiding the choices we make and the actions we take in our daily lives. Our beliefs about ourselves, others, and the world shape our self-image, relationships, career paths, and aspirations. For instance, someone who holds a belief in the power of perseverance and hard work is more likely to pursue their goals with determination and

persistence, while someone who doubts their abilities may sabotage their own success.

Graph: Beliefs and Behaviour

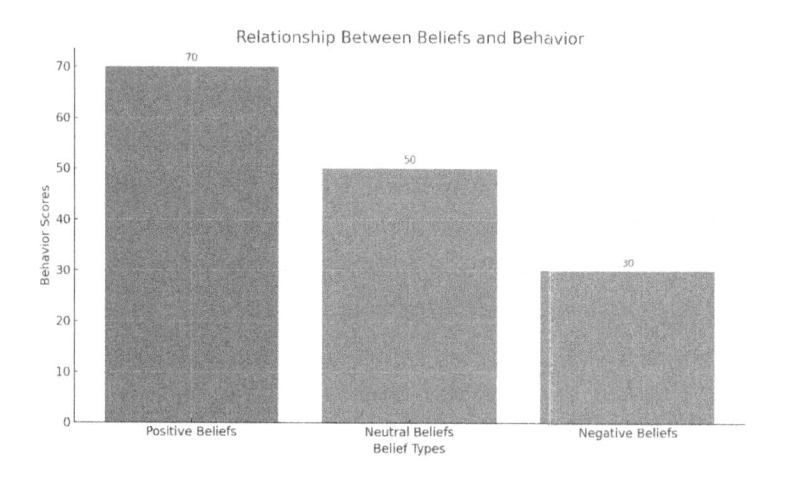

Figure 3: Bar graph illustrating the relationship between different types of beliefs (positive, neutral, and negative) and corresponding behaviour scores. The graph shows how positive beliefs are associated with higher behaviour scores, neutral beliefs with moderate scores, and negative beliefs with lower scores.

Self-Fulfilling Prophecies

Beliefs have the power to become self-fulfilling prophecies, influencing outcomes in accordance with our expectations. When we hold positive beliefs about ourselves and our capabilities, we are more likely to engage in behaviours that lead to success and fulfilment, thereby reinforcing our initial beliefs. Conversely, negative beliefs can create a self-perpetuating cycle of failure and disappointment, as our thoughts and actions align with our negative expectations.

Illustration: Self-Fulfilling Prophecy Cycle

An illustration of the self-fulfilling prophecy cycle:

Belief or Expectation:
A belief or expectation about a situation or person.

Behaviour or Action:
Behaviour towards the situation or person based on the belief.

Response or Reaction:
The situation or person responds or reacts to the behaviour.

Outcome:
The belief or expectation comes true due to the response. (Step 4 takes you back up to step 1, completing the Self-fulfilling Prophecy Cycle)

Graphically, this can be represented as a circle with arrows connecting each step to the next, emphasising the cyclical nature of the self-fulfilling prophecy.

Cycle of the Self-Fulfilling Prophecy

- Expectation
- Behavior
- Belief
- Outcome

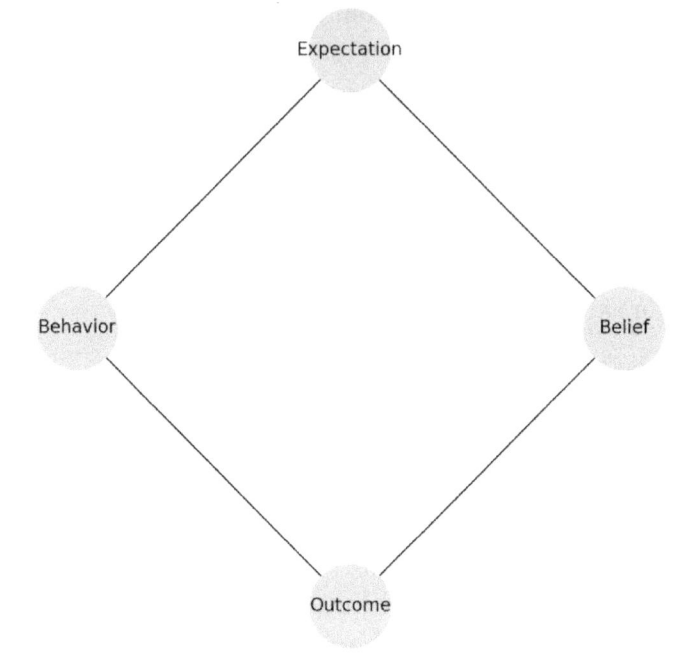

Figure 4: Cycle of Self-Fulfilling Prophecy

Here is a graphical representation of the cycle of the self-fulfilling prophecy, depicted as a circle with arrows connecting each step to the next. This illustration emphasises the cyclical nature of how beliefs lead to expectations, which influence behaviours, resulting in outcomes that reinforce the initial beliefs. The cycle continues as the outcome reinforces the original belief or expectation, perpetuating the self-fulfilling prophecy.

Resilience and Adaptability

Beliefs play a crucial role in fostering resilience and adaptability in the face of adversity. When you hold empowering beliefs about your ability to overcome challenges and learn from setbacks, you are better equipped to navigate life's ups and downs with more resilience. Reframing obstacles as opportunities for growth and learning, can transform setbacks into stepping stones for success. Some of the greatest lessons in life come during great adversity.

Table: Empowering vs. Limiting Beliefs

Empowering Beliefs	Limiting Beliefs
"I can learn from my mistakes."	"I always fail when I try."
"Every setback is a lesson."	"Setbacks are failures."
"I can adapt to new situations."	"Change is too difficult for me."

Shaping Reality and Manifestation

Beliefs have the power to shape our reality and influence the outcomes we manifest in our lives. Through the process of manifestation, our beliefs act as magnets, attracting people, opportunities, and circumstances that are in alignment with our dominant thoughts and emotions. By nurturing positive beliefs and maintaining a mindset of abundance and possibility, we can consciously co-create the reality we desire and manifest our deepest aspirations into existence. Remember, we all possess creative power.

Freedom and Empowerment

Ultimately, the power of belief lies in its ability to empower us to shape our own destinies and live authentically aligned lives. While external circumstances may be beyond our control, we have the freedom to choose our beliefs and perspectives in any given situation. Consciously choosing beliefs that uplift and empower us, helps us reclaim our agency and harness the transformative power of the mind to create a life of purpose.

Summary Table: The Power of Belief

Aspect	Positive Beliefs	Negative Beliefs
Perception	View challenges as opportunities	View challenges as threats
Behaviour	Proactive and goal-oriented	Avoidant and self-sabotaging
Self-Fulfilling Prophecy	Success reinforces belief in capability	Failure reinforces belief in incapability
Resilience	Bounce back and learn from setbacks	Struggle to recover and grow
Manifestation	Attract positive outcomes and opportunities	Attract negative outcomes and limitations
Empowerment	Feel empowered to shape destiny	Feel powerless and stuck

In essence, the power of belief is a potent force that shapes our thoughts, behaviours, and reality. By cultivating empowering beliefs and aligning our thoughts and actions with our deepest values and aspirations, we unlock the unlimited potential of the human spirit and embark on a journey of self-discovery, growth, and transformation.

8

The Art of Visualisation

The Art of Visualisation

The art of visualisation is a potent tool for harnessing the power of the mind to manifest our deepest desires and aspirations. Through vivid and detailed mental imagery, we create a bridge between the realm of thought and the realm of reality, allowing us to sculpt our future with intention and precision. Visualisation involves immersing ourselves in the sensory experience of our desired outcomes, seeing, feeling, and even hearing the manifestations of our dreams as if they were already a reality. By consistently and intentionally visualising our goals, we not only reinforce our beliefs in their attainment but also signal to the subconscious mind the direction in which we wish to journey. With each visualisation session, we cultivate a deeper sense of clarity, confidence, and conviction, empowering us to take inspired action towards the realisation of our deepest aspirations.

The art of visualisation is a potent practice that harnesses the creative power of the mind to manifest desired outcomes, cultivate inner clarity, and propel oneself towards success and fulfilment. It involves mentally imagining and vividly experiencing specific goals, experiences, or states of being with intention, focus, and emotional resonance. Here are some key insights into the art of visualisation:

Key Insights into the Art of Visualisation

Harnessing the Power of Imagination
Visualisation taps into the boundless potential of the imagination, allowing individuals to create detailed mental images and scenarios that represent their desired realities. By engaging the senses: sight, sound, touch, smell, taste, and proprioception; we bring our visions to life, making them feel vivid, tangible, and real in the inner landscape of the mind.

Sensory Engagement in Visualisation

Sense	Example in Visualisation
Sight	Visualising the appearance of a new home or office
Sound	Hearing the applause after a successful presentation
Touch	Feeling the texture of a diploma or award
Smell	Smelling the fresh air in a desired travel destination
Taste	Tasting the food at a celebratory meal
Proprioception	Moving hands and or arms with eyes closed to try and determine how far they are from your body

Creating a Blueprint for Success
Visualisation serves as a powerful tool for setting and achieving goals, as it enables individuals to create a mental blueprint of their desired outcomes. By visualising themselves succeeding, whether in their career, relationships,

health, or personal development, individuals prime their minds for success, aligning their thoughts, emotions, and actions with their goals.

Amplifying Focus and Clarity
Visualisation enhances mental focus and clarity, as it requires individuals to concentrate their attention on specific images, scenarios, or sensations. By repeatedly visualising their goals with clarity and precision, individuals clarify their intentions, strengthen their resolve, and sharpen their focus on what they want to achieve, thereby increasing their chances of success.

Illustration: Focus and Clarity Enhancement

Step	Description
Define Goal	Specify what you want to achieve
Create Mental Image	Visualise the goal with detailed imagery
Engage Emotions	Feel the emotions associated with success
Repeat Regularly	Practice visualisation daily
Track Progress	Monitor progress and adjust as needed

Programming the Subconscious Mind
Visualisation has the power to reprogram the subconscious mind, which governs a significant portion of our beliefs, attitudes, and behaviours. By consistently visualising positive outcomes and experiences, you can implant empowering suggestions into your subconscious, reinforcing your belief in

your ability to achieve your goals and overcome obstacles. This is essentially what faith is and how believing works.

Cultivating Emotional Resonance
Emotions play a crucial role in the process of visualisation, as they imbue our mental images with emotional resonance and intensity. By infusing your visualisations with positive emotions such as joy, gratitude, and confidence, you can amplify the energetic vibration of your desires, making you more magnetic and compelling to the universe. To enhance the effectiveness of visualisation, engage your emotions and tap into the feelings of joy, excitement, and fulfilment associated with achieving your goals. Allow yourself to experience the emotions of success as if they were already a reality, amplifying the positive energy and motivation driving you toward your desired outcomes.

Aligning with the Law of Attraction
Visualisation is closely aligned with the principles of the Law of Attraction, which states that 'like attracts like'. By visualising your desired outcomes as if they have already been achieved, you are sending out powerful energetic signals to the universe, drawing corresponding people, opportunities, and circumstances into your life. What you respect will gravitate towards you. Visualisation is a valuable tool for enhancing performance and skill acquisition in various domains, including sports, arts, and public speaking. Mentally rehearsing specific actions will prime your mind and body for

peak performance, building confidence, muscle memory, and neural pathways that support your goals and aspirations.

Create a Clear Mental Image
Once you've clarified your goals, create a clear mental image of what success looks like for you. Visualise yourself achieving your goals in vivid detail, engaging all your senses to make the experience as real and immersive as possible. Imagine the sights, sounds, smells, and sensations associated with your success, and allow yourself to fully experience the emotions of accomplishment and fulfilment. Before you can effectively visualise your desired outcomes, it's essential to clarify your goals and intentions. Take time to reflect on what you want to achieve, whether it's improving your performance in a particular area, achieving a specific milestone, or realising a long-term aspiration. Be specific and concrete in defining your goals, because the clearer they are, the higher your chances of achieving them.

Visualise both Obstacles and Solutions
In addition to visualising your successes, practice visualising potential obstacles or challenges you may encounter along the way. Imagine yourself overcoming these obstacles with resilience, creativity, and determination, finding solutions and forging ahead toward your goals despite setbacks. By mentally rehearsing your response to challenges, you can build confidence and resilience in the face of adversity. This also allows you a higher level of clarity of vision. Incorporate visualisation into your daily routine as a regular practice. Set

aside dedicated time each day to engage in visualisation exercises, preferably in a quiet and relaxing environment where you can focus your attention fully. Whether it's in the morning upon waking, during a meditation session, or before bedtime, find a time that works best for you and commit to practicing visualisation consistently.

Leave Room for Serendipity
While visualisation is a powerful tool for achieving your goals, it's crucial to stay open to unexpected opportunities and serendipitous events that may arise. Flexibility and adaptability in your approach allow you to be receptive to new possibilities and paths that might bring you closer to your objectives, even if they deviate from your original plan. Expectation is the birthplace of breakthroughs, so always anticipate positive outcomes. By harnessing the power of visualisation, you align your thoughts, emotions, and actions with your goals, accelerating your progress and amplifying your success. Through regular practice and commitment, visualisation can become a transformative tool for overcoming obstacles to creating your ideal life.

Essentially, the art of visualisation empowers you to harness your mind's creative power and manifest your deepest aspirations. By cultivating the ability to visualise with clarity, intention, and emotion, you will unlock the unlimited potential of your imagination and embark on a journey of self-discovery, and significant growth. By harnessing the power of visualisation, you align your thoughts, emotions, and actions with your goals, accelerating your progress and amplifying your success. Regular practice and commitment make visualisation a transformative tool for manifesting dreams, overcoming obstacles, and creating the desired life. The art of visualisation empowers individuals to harness the mind's creative power, unlocking the unlimited potential of imagination and embarking on a journey of self-discovery, growth, and fulfilment.

9

Cultivating a Positive Mindset

Cultivating a Positive Mindset

Cultivating a positive mindset is akin to tending to a garden; it requires nurturing, attention, and intentionality to flourish. It involves consciously choosing to focus on the bright side of life, even in the face of adversity. By reframing challenges as opportunities for growth, setbacks as lessons in resilience, and failures as stepping stones to success, we shift our perspective from one of limitation to one of boundless possibility. Having a positive mindset is not about denying the existence of negativity or avoiding difficult emotions; rather, it's about embracing the full spectrum of human experience while consciously choosing to dwell in the realm of optimism and gratitude. Through practices such as affirmations, gratitude journaling, and positive self-talk, we train our minds to seek out the silver linings in every situation, fostering resilience, and unlocking the door to a life of joy and abundance.

Possessing a positive mindset is a transformative practice that empowers you to approach life with optimism, resilience, and gratitude, thereby enhancing your overall well-being and success. It involves adopting a mental attitude characterised by positivity, hope, and a belief in your ability to overcome challenges and thrive in any situation. Surround yourself with positivity, because the company you keep has a significant impact on your mindset and outlook on life. This can be through relationships, media consumption, or daily habits. By intentionally choosing to spend time with people who inspire and uplift us, we reinforce our own positive mindset and energy. Here are some key insights into the practice of cultivating a positive mindset:

Shifting Perspectives
Cultivating a positive mindset begins with a conscious shift in perspective. This involves reframing challenges as opportunities for growth and learning. Instead of focusing on obstacles and limitations, you can with a positive mindset choose to see setbacks as temporary and as stepping stones towards your goals.

Illustration: Perspective Shift

Situation	Negative Perspective	Positive Perspective
Job Rejection	"I'm not good enough."	"This is a chance to find a better fit."
Failed Project	"I'm a failure."	"I learned valuable lessons for next time."
Personal Conflict	"This relationship is doomed."	"We have an opportunity to strengthen our bond."

Fostering Gratitude and Appreciation
Gratitude is a cornerstone of a positive mindset, as it encourages individuals to focus on the abundance and blessings in their lives rather than dwelling on what they lack. By cultivating a daily practice of gratitude, whether through journaling, reflection, or verbal affirmations, you can train your mind to notice and appreciate the goodness that surrounds you.

Table: Benefits of Gratitude

Benefit	Description
Enhanced Well-Being	Improved overall happiness and life satisfaction.
Reduced Stress	Lower levels of stress and anxiety.
Better Relationships	Strengthened social connections and empathy.

Nurturing Self-Compassion and Self-Love

A positive mindset involves treating oneself with kindness, compassion, and self-love, especially during times of difficulty or adversity. Instead of engaging in self-criticism or negative self-talk, you maintain a positive mindset and practice self-compassion, acknowledging your imperfections and mistakes with understanding and forgiveness.

Illustration: Self-Compassion Practice

Situation	Self-Critical Response	Self-Compassionate Response
Making a Mistake	"I'm so stupid."	"Everyone makes mistakes; it's okay to learn."
Feeling Overwhelmed	"I can't handle this."	"I'm doing my best, and it's okay to take a break."
Facing Rejection	"I'm not worth it."	"This doesn't define my value as a person."

Focusing on Solutions and Possibilities

When you have a positive mindset, you will approach challenges with a solution-focused mindset, seeking opportunities for growth and creative problem-solving. Instead of dwelling on problems or obstacles, you channel your energy into identifying actionable steps and solutions that move you closer to your goals.

Table: Positive Influences

Positive Influence	Description
Supportive Friends	Encouraging and uplifting social interactions.
Inspiring Content	Consuming motivational and educational media.
Healthy Habits	Engaging in activities that promote well-being.

Table: Solution-Focused Approach

Challenge	Problem-Focused Approach	Solution-Focused Approach
Tight Deadline	"There's not enough time."	"What steps can I take to manage my time effectively?"
Budget Cuts	"We can't afford this project."	"How can we achieve our goals within the new budget?"
Team Conflict	"Our team isn't working well together."	"What can we do to improve communication and teamwork?"

In essence, cultivating a positive mindset is a transformative practice that empowers you to approach life with optimism, resilience, and gratitude, thereby enhancing your overall well-being and success. It involves adopting a mental attitude characterised by positivity, hope, and a belief in one's ability to overcome challenges and thrive in any situation. When you consciously choose positivity, you unlock the door to a life that transcends your earthly existance.

10

The Power of Affirmations

The Power of Affirmations

The power of affirmations lies in their ability to reprogram the subconscious mind, reshaping our beliefs, attitudes, and behaviours to align with our deepest desires and aspirations. Affirmations are positive statements that we repeat to ourselves consistently, with the intention of reinforcing empowering beliefs and manifesting our goals into reality. By affirming our inherent worthiness, capability, and potential, we cultivate a mindset of self-belief and confidence that propels us towards success. Whether spoken aloud, written down, or silently whispered, affirmations have the remarkable ability to shift our internal dialogue from one of self-doubt and limitation to one of empowerment and possibility. With each repetition, we plant seeds of positivity in the fertile soil of our subconscious, paving the way for transformation, growth, and abundance in all areas of our lives.

The power of affirmations lies in their ability to reprogram the subconscious mind, shaping our beliefs, thoughts, and behaviours in alignment with our deepest desires and aspirations. Affirmations are positive statements or declarations that are consciously chosen and repeated regularly to manifest specific outcomes in our lives.

How Affirmations Work

Reprogramming the Subconscious Mind
Affirmations influence the subconscious mind, which controls a significant portion of our beliefs, attitudes, and behaviours. By repeating positive statements aligned with our goals, we imprint these affirmations onto our subconscious, replacing limiting beliefs and negative self-talk with empowering and supportive messages. With undivided focus consistency, your new way of thinking will become your natural inclination and way of life.

Example Affirmations

Area of Life	Affirmation Example
Self-Esteem	"I am worthy of love and respect."
Career	"I am capable and confident in my professional skills."
Health	"I am healthy, energetic, and full of vitality."
Relationships	"I attract positive and loving relationships into my life."

Principles of the Law of Attraction
Affirmations align with the principles of the Law of Attraction, which states that like attracts like. By focusing our thoughts and intentions on what we want to manifest, rather than what we lack or fear, we align ourselves with the energetic frequency of our desires, drawing corresponding people, opportunities, and circumstances into our lives.

Promoting Positive Self-Talk

Affirmations foster positive self-talk and self-validation, encouraging a mindset of self-love, worthiness, and empowerment. Instead of succumbing to self-doubt or criticism, affirmations empower us to speak to ourselves with kindness, compassion, and encouragement, reinforcing our belief in our own abilities and worth.

Table: Positive vs. Negative Self-Talk

Situation	Negative Self-Talk	Positive Affirmation
Facing a Challenge	"I can't do this."	"I am capable and can overcome this."
Making a Mistake	"I always mess up."	"I learn and grow from my experiences."
Feeling Overwhelmed	"This is too much for me."	"I manage my tasks with ease and grace."

Boosting Confidence and Self-Efficacy

Regular practice of affirmations boosts confidence and self-efficacy, leading to bolstering our confidence to take bold actions, pursue our goals, and overcome obstacles with resilience and determination.

Shifting Beliefs and Perspectives

Affirmations shift our beliefs and perspectives, transforming limiting beliefs into empowering ones and reframing challenges as opportunities for growth. Consistent repetition of affirmations helps create new neural pathways in the brain that support success and well-being.

Table: Transforming Limiting Beliefs

Limiting Belief	Empowering Affirmation
"I'm not good enough."	"I am more than enough."
"Success is for others."	"I create my own success."
"I can't change."	"I am capable of growth and transformation."

Enhancing Emotional Resilience and Well-Being

Affirmations enhance emotional resilience and well-being by promoting a positive outlook on life and fostering a sense of inner peace and contentment. Train mind to see beauty and abundance even amidst adversity.

Example Affirmations for Emotional Resilience

Affirmation	Purpose
"I am grateful for all the good in my life."	Cultivates gratitude
"I face challenges with courage and strength."	Builds resilience
"I am surrounded by love and support."	Enhances emotional well-being

Integrating Affirmations into Daily Routines

To harness the full power of affirmations, it's important to integrate them into daily rituals and routines. Whether through morning affirmations, journaling, or visualisation exercises, consistent practice reinforces the messages and beliefs we seek to embody and become.

Table: Daily Affirmation Practices

Practice	Description	Example Affirmation
Morning Affirmations	Start your day with positive statements	"Today, I am focused and productive."
Journaling	Write down affirmations and reflect on them	"I am grateful for my progress."
Visualisation Exercises	Visualise affirmations manifesting in reality	"I see myself achieving my goals with ease."

The power of affirmations lies in their ability to reprogram the subconscious mind, aligning our thoughts, beliefs, and behaviours with our deepest desires and aspirations. By harnessing the transformative power of affirmations, we empower ourselves to create lives filled with joy, abundance, and personal satisfaction. Consistent practice of affirmations can shift our internal dialogue from self-doubt and limitation to empowerment and possibility, leading to profound personal growth and success.

11

Embracing the Journey

Embracing the Journey

Embracing the journey is about surrendering to the flow of life and recognising that the path to growth and fulfilment is as important as the destination itself. It entails embracing the ups and downs, twists and turns, joys and sorrows that come with navigating the human experience. Rather than fixating on the end goal, embracing the journey invites us to savour each moment, finding beauty and meaning in the present. It's about cultivating a mindset of curiosity, resilience, and gratitude as we navigate the unknown terrain of life, trusting that every experience, whether pleasant or challenging, serves as a valuable lesson and opportunity for growth. As we approach life with an open heart and a courageous spirit, we tap into the transformative power of the present moment, allowing it to shape us into our best selves.

A Transformative Practice
This way of life is a transformative practice that invites you to fully engage with the unfolding process of life, embracing both its challenges and blessings with openness, curiosity, and gratitude. Rather than fixating solely on the destination or end goal, embracing the journey involves appreciating the richness and beauty of each moment along the way. Here are some key insights into the practice of embracing the journey:

Cultivating Present-Moment Awareness
Embracing the journey begins with cultivating present-moment awareness, anchoring oneself in the here and now

with mindfulness and intention. By consciously attuning our attention to the present moment, we become fully immersed in the richness of our experiences, whether mundane or extraordinary. This presence allows us to cultivate a deep sense of gratitude for the gift of life and the unfolding journey.

Letting Go of Attachment to Outcomes
Embracing the journey requires letting go of attachment to specific outcomes or expectations. It involves allowing life to unfold organically, without rigid control. Instead of obsessing over the future or dwelling on the past, we surrender to the natural flow of life, trusting in the wisdom of the universe and embracing the unknown with faith and surrender. This frees us from unnecessary stress and opens us to new possibilities.

Embracing Change
Life is inherently impermanent and ever-changing. Embracing the journey means embracing the inevitability of change as an essential aspect of growth and transformation. Rather than resisting or fearing change, we welcome new experiences and opportunities for expansion with an open heart and mind. Every step of the journey offers an opportunity for growth, learning, and self-discovery, contributing to our personal evolution and awakening.

Navigating Challenges with Resilience
Challenges and obstacles are an inherent part of the journey, serving as opportunities for growth, resilience, and self-discovery. Embracing the journey involves meeting

challenges with courage, resilience, and grace. Trusting in our inner strength and wisdom, we navigate adversity and emerge stronger and more empowered on the other side. Each challenge faced and overcome becomes a testament to our resilience and a stepping stone to our growth.

Celebrating Milestones and Victories
While embracing the journey involves staying present and open to the process, it's also important to celebrate milestones and victories along the way. Acknowledging and honouring our progress and accomplishments, no matter how small, develops a sense of joy, and appreciation for the journey itself. And celebrating these moments reinforces our commitment to the path and provides motivation to keep going.

The Spirit of Adventure and Exploration
Embracing the journey is akin to embarking on a grand adventure, full of surprises, discoveries, and opportunities for growth. Approach life with curiosity, wonder, and a willingness to step outside of your comfort zones. This openness allows you to embrace new experiences and possibilities, enriching your journey with diversity and depth. In essence, embracing the journey is a transformative practice that invites individuals to fully engage with the richness and complexity of life. Let go of attachment to outcomes and find meaning in the process itself. This awakening to the beauty and sacredness of the journey allows us to reclaim our innate sense of wonder and awe for the miracle of existence.

12

The Power of Neuroplasticity

The Power of Neuroplasticity

Neuroplasticity, the brain's remarkable ability to reorganise itself by forming new neural connections throughout life, is a fundamental concept in understanding how we can transform our thinking and behaviour. This concept underpins the idea that our brains are not static but dynamic, capable of change and adaptation in response to new experiences, learning, and even injury. In this chapter, we will explore the power of neuroplasticity and how it can be harnessed for personal growth and transformation. Practical illustrations will help to elucidate these concepts and provide understanding.

Exploring the Brain's Capacity for Change

The human brain, with its intricate network of neurons and synapses, is a marvel of adaptability and resilience. For decades, scientists believed that the brain's structure and function were fixed beyond early childhood. However, groundbreaking research in the field of neuroscience has revealed the remarkable capacity of the brain to change and rewire itself in response to experience, a phenomenon known as neuroplasticity. One of the most fascinating aspects of neuroplasticity is its role in shaping our thoughts, beliefs, and emotions. Studies have shown that our experiences and mental activities can physically alter the structure and function of the brain, leading to changes in behaviour, perception, and cognition. For example, practicing mindfulness meditation has been found to increase the density of gray matter in brain regions associated with attention, memory, and emotional regulation.

Furthermore, neuroplasticity is not limited to specific areas of the brain but is a widespread phenomenon that can occur throughout the entire nervous system. This means that the brain has the capacity to adapt and change in response to a wide range of stimuli, from learning a new language to recovering from a traumatic injury. Understanding the brain's capacity for change opens exciting possibilities for personal growth, healing, and transformation. It suggests that we are not limited by our past experiences or genetic predispositions but have the power to shape our own destinies through conscious effort and intention. By harnessing the principles of neuroplasticity, we can cultivate new habits, rewire negative thought patterns, heal from our past, and unlock our full potential for creativity, resilience, and overall well-being.

In the pages that follow, we will explore practical strategies for harnessing the power of neuroplasticity to optimise brain health, enhance cognitive function, and promote emotional well-being. By understanding and leveraging the brain's capacity for change, we can embark on a journey of self-discovery and empowerment, unlocking new levels of vitality. Reshaping the anatomy of your brain with your mind is an awe-inspiring concept that highlights the extraordinary capacity of the human brain for adaptation and change. While the physical structure of the brain may seem fixed, emerging research in neuroscience has revealed that our thoughts, emotions, and experiences can profoundly influence its anatomy and function.

Types of Neuroplasticity

Functional Plasticity: The brain's ability to move functions from damaged areas to undamaged areas.

Structural Plasticity: The brain's ability to physically change its structure in response to learning, experience, or injury.

Illustration: Types of Neuroplasticity

Type	Description	Example
Functional Plasticity	Reassignment of functions to different brain areas	Recovering speech after a stroke
Structural Plasticity	Physical changes in brain structure due to new experiences	Enlarged hippocampus in taxi drivers

The Mechanisms of Neuroplasticity

Synaptic Plasticity
Synaptic plasticity involves changes in the strength of connections between neurons. Long-term potentiation (LTP) and long-term depression (LTD) are two primary processes:

LTP: Strengthening of synapses based on recent patterns of activity.

LTD: Weakening of synapses that results from low-frequency stimulation.

Neurogenesis
Neurogenesis is the process by which new neurons are formed in the brain. This process predominantly occurs in the hippocampus, a region associated with learning and memory.

The Power of Neurogenesis
Neurogenesis, the process of generating new neurons in the brain, is a remarkable facet of neuroplasticity that has profound implications for learning, memory, mood regulation, and overall brain health. Understanding and leveraging neurogenesis can significantly enhance our cognitive abilities and emotional well-being. This chapter will look into the science of neurogenesis, its benefits, and practical ways to stimulate it, illustrated with tables.

Understanding Neurogenesis

What is Neurogenesis?
Neurogenesis is the birth of new neurons from neural stem cells and progenitor cells in the brain. This process predominantly occurs in two brain regions:

Hippocampus: Critical for learning and memory.

Subventricular Zone (SVZ): Involved in olfactory function.

Illustration: Brain Regions of Neurogenesis

Brain Region	Function	Neurogenesis Activity
Hippocampus	Learning, memory, emotion regulation	High
Subventricular Zone	Olfactory function, neural repair	Moderate

Benefits of Neurogenesis
Neurogenesis is crucial for several brain functions and overall mental health.

Table: Benefits of Neurogenesis

Benefit	Description	Supporting Evidence
Learning and Memory	Enhances cognitive functions and adaptability	Studies on hippocampal neurogenesis
Mood Regulation	Reduces symptoms of depression and anxiety	Research on antidepressant effects
Cognitive Resilience	Protects against age-related cognitive decline	Longitudinal studies on brain health

Learning and Memory: New neurons enhance cognitive flexibility and the ability to learn new information.

Mood Regulation: Neurogenesis in the hippocampus is linked to emotional regulation and has implications for treating depression and anxiety.

Cognitive Resilience: Increased neurogenesis can help protect the brain from age-related decline and neurodegenerative diseases.

Factors Influencing Neurogenesis
Several lifestyle factors can either enhance or inhibit neurogenesis:

Enhancers

Physical Exercise: Aerobic exercises like running stimulate the production of new neurons.
Diet: Nutrients such as omega-3 fatty acids, flavonoids, and curcumin promote neurogenesis.
Mental Stimulation: Learning new skills and engaging in challenging mental activities enhance neurogenesis.
Sleep: Quality sleep is crucial for neurogenesis and overall brain function.
Stress Management: Chronic stress inhibits neurogenesis, so stress reduction techniques are beneficial.

Inhibitors

Chronic Stress: Prolonged stress reduces neurogenesis and negatively impacts brain health.
Poor Diet: Diets high in sugar and saturated fats can inhibit neurogenesis.
Lack of Sleep: Sleep deprivation impairs neurogenesis and cognitive function.

Practical Ways to Stimulate Neurogenesis

Physical Exercise

Regular aerobic exercise, such as running or cycling, is one of the most effective ways to boost neurogenesis. Aim for at least 150 minutes of moderate aerobic activity or 75 minutes of vigorous activity each week. Physical exercise has been shown to have profound effects on brain health and neuroplasticity. Aerobic exercise promotes the release of growth factors that stimulate the growth of new neurons and the formation of new synapses. Additionally, exercise increases blood flow to the brain, providing it with the oxygen and nutrients it needs to function optimally. Incorporate activities such as walking, running, swimming, or yoga into your daily routine to promote the release of growth factors that stimulate the growth of new neurons and synapses. Aim for at least 30 minutes of moderate intensity exercise most days of the week to support optimal brain function and cognitive vitality. Remember to keep it moving.

Diet
A healthy diet rich in antioxidants, omega-3 fatty acids, and other nutrients is essential for supporting brain health and neuroplasticity. Foods such as fruits, vegetables, fatty fish, nuts, and seeds provide the building blocks necessary for the growth and repair of brain cells, while minimising consumption of processed foods and sugars can help protect against inflammation and oxidative stress, which can impair neuroplasticity. What we consume affects us a great deal.

Incorporating these strategies into our daily lives can help us harness the power of neuroplasticity to optimise brain health, enhance cognitive function, and promote emotional well-being. By nurturing our brains with stimulating activities, healthy habits, and a supportive environment, we can unlock our full potential and cultivate a thriving mind-body connection that supports us in living our best lives.
Include brain-boosting foods into your diet such as:

Omega-3 Fatty Acids:
Found in fatty fish, flaxseeds, and walnuts.
Flavonoids:
Present in dark chocolate, blueberries, and green tea.
Curcumin:
The active ingredient in turmeric.

Table: Diet and Neurogenesis

Nutrient	Food Sources	Benefits for Neurogenesis
Omega-3 Fatty Acids	Fatty fish, flaxseeds, walnuts	Enhances neuron formation and function
Flavonoids	Dark chocolate, blueberries, green tea	Promotes brain health and cognitive function
Curcumin	Turmeric	Stimulates neurogenesis and reduces inflammation

Mental Stimulation

Engage in activities that challenge your brain, such as learning a new language, playing a musical instrument, or solving puzzles. These activities can stimulate the growth of new neurons and improve cognitive function. Engaging in activities that challenge and stimulate the brain, such as puzzles, brainteasers, and memory games, can promote neuroplasticity by strengthening neural connections and increasing cognitive reserve. Regularly exposing the brain to new and complex stimuli, encourages the growth of new neurons and synapses, leading to improved cognitive function and resilience. There are numerous brain training apps available that offer a variety of exercises designed to challenge and stimulate the brain. These apps often include games and puzzles that target cognitive functions such as memory, attention, and problem-solving.

Neurofeedback Training
Neurofeedback is a form of biofeedback that uses real-time brain activity measurements to help individuals learn to regulate their brain function. During a neurofeedback session, sensors are placed on the scalp to monitor brainwave activity, and feedback is provided to the individual in the form of visual or auditory cues. Learning to modulate your brainwave patterns, will help to promote changes in brain function and improve symptoms associated with conditions such as anxiety, depression, and ADHD.

Sleep
Prioritise getting 7-9 hours of quality sleep per night to support neurogenesis and overall brain health. Establish a regular sleep schedule and create a restful environment to enhance sleep quality. Adequate sleep is essential for brain health and neuroplasticity. During sleep, the brain consolidates memories, clears out toxins, and undergoes important repair processes. Chronic sleep deprivation has been shown to impair neuroplasticity and cognitive function, while quality sleep supports optimal brain function and promotes neuroplasticity.

Stress Management
Practice stress-reducing techniques such as mindfulness meditation, yoga, and deep-breathing exercises. Reducing

stress can help promote neurogenesis and improve mental well-being. Mindfulness meditation is a powerful practice for promoting neuroplasticity and cultivating emotional well-being. Regular practice has been shown to increase gray matter density in brain regions associated with these functions, leading to improvements in mood, stress resilience, and overall mental health. Mindfulness meditation is a powerful practice for rewiring the brain and promoting emotional well-being. Begin by finding a quiet, comfortable space and sitting or lying down in a relaxed position. Close your eyes and bring your attention to your breath, noticing the sensation of each inhale and exhale. As thoughts arise, simply observe them without judgment and gently bring your focus back to your breath. With regular practice, mindfulness meditation can strengthen neural pathways associated with attention, emotional regulation, and self-awareness, leading to greater resilience and well-being.

Practical Applications of Neuroplasticity

Learning and Skill Acquisition
Chronic stress and negative emotions can have detrimental effects on brain structure and function, contributing to shrinkage in key regions such as the hippocampus and prefrontal cortex. In contrast, practices that promote emotional regulation, such as cognitive-behavioural therapy and relaxation techniques, can mitigate the impact of stress on the brain and promote neuroplasticity. Lifelong learning is one of the most effective ways to promote neuroplasticity and

enhance brain health. Whether it's learning a new language, musical instrument, or skill, engaging in novel and intellectually stimulating activities stimulates the brain's plasticity, fostering the growth of new neural networks and enhancing cognitive flexibility.

Engaging in activities that require learning new skills, such as playing a musical instrument, learning a new language, or mastering a new hobby, can promote neuroplasticity by stimulating the growth of new neural connections. Choose a skill that interests you and commit to practicing it regularly, challenging yourself to progress and improve over time. Not only will you expand your skillset, but you'll also strengthen your brain's ability to adapt and learn new information.

Table: Steps for Skill Acquisition Through Neuroplasticity

Step	Description	Example Activity
Repetition	Consistent practice strengthens neural pathways	Daily language practice
Incremental Progress	Gradually increasing difficulty enhances learning	Progressive musical exercises
Feedback	Receiving feedback helps refine skills	Teacher or peer reviews

Rehabilitation and Recovery

Neuroplasticity plays a vital role in recovery from brain injuries. Through targeted therapies and exercises, individuals can regain lost functions.

Case Study: Stroke Rehabilitation

A study of stroke patients showed significant recovery in motor functions through neuroplastic interventions.

Mental Health and Emotional Well-Being

Neuroplasticity also affects mental health. Practices such as mindfulness, cognitive-behavioural therapy (CBT), and meditation can lead to structural and functional changes in the brain that enhance emotional well-being.

Table: Neuroplastic Practices for Mental Health

Practice	Description	Brain Area Affected
Mindfulness Meditation	Enhances attention and emotional regulation	Prefrontal cortex, amygdala
CBT	Reframes negative thinking patterns	Prefrontal cortex
Physical Exercise	Increases neurogenesis and overall brain health	Hippocampus

Harnessing Neuroplasticity

Developing a Growth Mindset
Adopting a growth mindset, the belief that abilities and intelligence can be developed, is foundational for leveraging neuroplasticity for personal growth.

Steps to Enhance Neuroplasticity

Engage in Novel Experiences: Continuously challenge your brain with new activities.

Practice Regular Physical Exercise: Exercise boosts brain health and neurogenesis.

Maintain a Healthy Diet: Nutrients like omega-3 fatty acids support brain function.

Prioritise Sleep: Quality sleep is essential for memory consolidation and brain health.

Manage Stress: Chronic stress impairs neuroplasticity, engage in stress-reducing activities.

Visualisation: Take a few minutes each day to visualise yourself successfully achieving your goals, whether it's giving a confident presentation, or acing an exam. Imagine yourself in vivid detail, engaging all your senses and emotions as you visualise your desired outcome. With regular practice, visualisation can strengthen neural pathways associated with goal achievement and increase your likelihood of success. As we cultivate habits that promote neuroplasticity such as visualisation, we set the stage for ongoing transformation and lifelong learning.

Table: Daily Routine for Enhancing Neuroplasticity

Time of Day	Activity	Neuroplastic Benefit
Morning	Mindfulness Meditation	Enhances attention and emotional regulation
Afternoon	Physical Exercise	Increases neurogenesis and overall brain health
Evening	Learning a New Skill	Strengthens new neural pathways
Night	Quality Sleep	Facilitates memory consolidation

13

Brain Physiology & Transformational Thinking

Understanding the Physiology of the Brain in Relation to Transformational Thinking

Understanding the brain's physiology is fundamental to unlocking the potential of transformational thinking. By comprehending how various brain structures and processes contribute to our thoughts, emotions, and behaviours, we can harness this knowledge to foster personal growth, resilience, and positive change. This chapter looks into the key brain regions and physiological processes involved in transformational thinking, illustrated with tables for clarity.

Key Brain Regions Involved in Transformational Thinking

1. Prefrontal Cortex
The prefrontal cortex (PFC) is crucial for higher-order cognitive functions such as decision-making, planning, and impulse control. It plays a pivotal role in transformational thinking by enabling us to set goals, envision future possibilities, and regulate our behaviours to achieve desired outcomes.

2. Hippocampus
The hippocampus is essential for learning and memory. It helps us retain new information and draw upon past experiences to inform our decisions and actions. In transformational thinking, the hippocampus aids in

integrating new knowledge and experiences, allowing us to adapt and grow.

3. Amygdala
The amygdala is involved in emotional processing and response. It plays a role in detecting threats and generating emotional reactions. While often associated with fear and stress, the amygdala is also important for emotional learning and resilience, critical components of transformational thinking.

4. Basal Ganglia
The basal ganglia are involved in habit formation and procedural learning. They help automate repetitive behaviours, freeing up cognitive resources for more complex tasks. Understanding the role of the basal ganglia in habit formation can aid in transforming negative habits into positive ones.

5. Anterior Cingulate Cortex
The anterior cingulate cortex (ACC) is involved in error detection, emotional regulation, and cognitive flexibility. It helps us adapt to changing circumstances and overcome obstacles, making it essential for transformational thinking.

Table: Brain Regions and Their Roles in Transformational Thinking

Brain Region	Primary Function	Role in Transformational Thinking
Prefrontal Cortex (PFC)	Decision-making, planning, impulse control	Goal setting, envisioning possibilities
Hippocampus	Learning, memory	Integrating new knowledge, adaptation
Amygdala	Emotional processing, response	Emotional learning, resilience
Basal Ganglia	Habit formation, procedural learning	Transforming habits
Anterior Cingulate Cortex (ACC)	Error detection, emotional regulation, cognitive flexibility	Adaptation, overcoming obstacles

Neuroplasticity and Neurogenesis

Neuroplasticity - Neuroplasticity refers to the brain's ability to reorganise itself by forming new neural connections throughout life. This adaptability is crucial for learning, memory, and recovery from brain injuries. Neuroplasticity underpins transformational thinking by allowing the brain to adapt to new information, experiences, and challenges.

Neurogenesis - Neurogenesis is the process of generating new neurons, particularly in the hippocampus. This process contributes to learning, memory, and emotional regulation. Enhancing neurogenesis through lifestyle choices such as exercise, diet, and mental stimulation can support transformational thinking.

Graph: Neuroplasticity and Neurogenesis Over Time

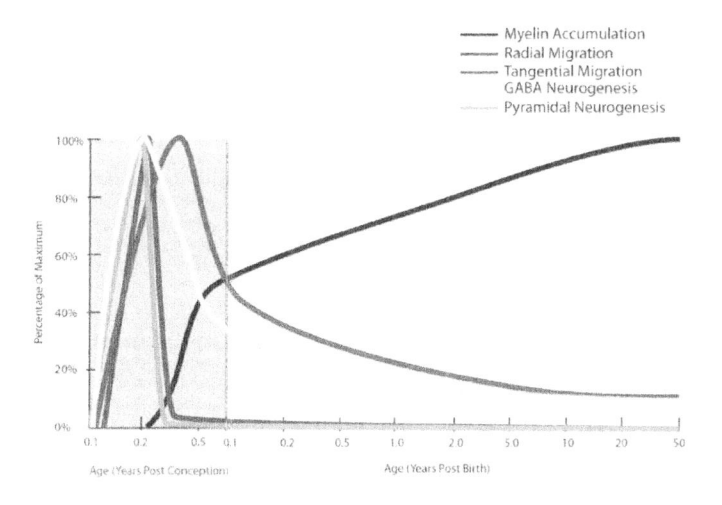

Figure 5: Graph showing Neuroplasticity and Neurogenesis over time (Image source - ResearchGate.)

The Role of Neurotransmitters

Dopamine - Dopamine is a neurotransmitter associated with motivation, reward, and pleasure. It plays a crucial role in goal-directed behaviour and reinforcement learning, making it essential for maintaining motivation and focus during transformational thinking.

Serotonin - Serotonin is linked to mood regulation, well-being, and emotional stability. Adequate serotonin levels are important for maintaining a positive mindset and emotional resilience, both of which are critical for transformational thinking.

Cortisol - Cortisol is a hormone released in response to stress. While short-term cortisol release can enhance performance and focus, chronic stress and elevated cortisol levels can impair cognitive function and emotional regulation. Managing stress is therefore essential for effective transformational thinking and will prove to be critical throughout your journey to success and self-actualisation.

Table: Neurotransmitters and Their Roles in Transformational Thinking

Neurotransmitter	Primary Function	Role in Transformational Thinking
Dopamine	Motivation, reward, pleasure	Goal-directed behaviour, reinforcement learning
Serotonin	Mood regulation, well-being, emotional stability	Positive mindset, emotional resilience
Cortisol	Stress response	Short-term focus, managing chronic stress

Practical Applications for Enhancing Transformational Thinking

1. Physical Exercise
Regular aerobic exercise can enhance neurogenesis and neuroplasticity, improving cognitive function and emotional well-being. Exercise also increases dopamine and serotonin levels, supporting motivation and mood regulation.

2. Mindfulness and Meditation
Practicing mindfulness and meditation can strengthen the prefrontal cortex and ACC, enhancing cognitive flexibility, emotional regulation, and stress management. These practices can also lower cortisol levels, reducing the impact of chronic stress.

3. Cognitive Training
Engaging in cognitive training exercises, such as puzzles, learning new skills, and problem-solving activities, can stimulate neuroplasticity and improve cognitive function. These activities can help rewire the brain for effective transformational thinking.

4. Diet and Nutrition
Consuming a diet rich in omega-3 fatty acids, antioxidants, and other brain-boosting nutrients can support neurogenesis and overall brain health. Foods such as fatty fish, blueberries, and turmeric can enhance cognitive function and emotional

well-being. Overall, a balanced diet is key to successful transformational thinking.

Understanding the physiology of the brain provides invaluable insights into the mechanisms underlying transformational thinking. By leveraging knowledge of brain regions, neuroplasticity, neurotransmitters, and practical applications, we can cultivate a mindset conducive to personal growth and positive change. Embracing practices that enhance brain health and function opens the door to a more fulfilling and empowered life, guided by the principles of transformational thinking. Through regular exercise, mindfulness practices, cognitive training, and a brain-healthy diet, we can harness the full potential of our brains, fostering resilience, creativity, and the ability to thrive in the face of challenges.

Table: Practical Applications for Enhancing Transformational Thinking

Practice	Benefits	Supporting Evidence
Physical Exercise	Enhances neurogenesis, improves mood	Studies on exercise and brain health
Mindfulness/ Meditation	Strengthens PFC and ACC, lowers cortisol	Research on mindfulness and cognitive function
Cognitive Training	Stimulates neuroplasticity, improves cognition	Studies on brain training exercises
Diet and Nutrition	Supports neurogenesis, boosts brain health	Research on diet and cognitive function

14

Building New Neuro Pathways

Success By Neuro Design

Success is not an accident, it involves being inconvenienced sometimes, it is a combination of consistent actions that you take every day. It comes with focussing on your goals and staying hungry and making your daily routines line up with your goals. Imagine you find yourself in a dense forest, full of untamed and overgrown bushes. If you grew up in Africa, like I did, this will be easy for you to imagine, as we walked places like this many times in our youth. You need to get to a clearing on the other side, but there is no clear path. The first time you walk through, it's tough. You push aside branches, trample down undergrowth, and mark the way as you go. It's slow, difficult work, but with each step, you're creating a trail; you are creating a path literally from nowhere.

Each time you take the same path, it becomes a bit easier. The bushes stay pushed aside, the ground becomes firmer, and soon you have a clear trail that you can walk without thinking. This well-trodden path represents the formation of a new neural pathway in your brain. By repeatedly thinking in a certain way or performing a specific action, you're creating and reinforcing this pathway.

Now, let's say you stop using this path and take a different route instead. Over time, the original path begins to fade. The bushes grow back, and the trail becomes indistinguishable from the surrounding forest. Similarly, if you stop using a particular neural pathway; say, a habit or a thought pattern, it will weaken and eventually become overgrown, making it harder to follow.

In the same way, by training our brain to think or act in new ways, we create new neural pathways. Consistent action and repeated practice keep these new pathways clear and strong. When you decide to adopt a new habit or learn a new skill, it's like walking that new path in the forest. At first, it may feel challenging and unnatural, but with persistence, the path becomes clearer and easier to navigate.

This process of creating new neural pathways is driven by the brain's neuroplasticity, which is its ability to reorganise itself by forming new neural connections. As you engage in new behaviours or think in new ways, you're giving your brain instructions to shape itself accordingly. These new pathways start to inform your behaviour automatically, making the new habits feel natural and ingrained.

Over time, the physical structure of your brain changes. Just as the forest path becomes a clear road, your brain's neural network becomes more efficient and organised to support the new behaviour. This leads to lasting changes in behaviour, as your brain now takes instruction from the mind's new patterns and preferences.

In essence, by consistently practicing new ways of thinking and acting, you're not just forming new pathways in the brain but are reshaping the landscape of your mind. This transformation is enduring, allowing new behaviours and habits to become a permanent part of who you are. This is a wonderful realisation because it means people can change.

Understanding Neural Pathways and Behaviour

Neural pathways are intricate networks of interconnected neurons that transmit information throughout the brain and nervous system. These pathways play a fundamental role in shaping our thoughts, emotions, and behaviours, serving as the biological basis for our cognitive processes and actions. In this section, we will explore the structure and function of neural pathways and their influence on behaviour.

Structure of Neural Pathways

Neural pathways consist of bundles of nerve fibres, known as axons, that connect different regions of the brain and spinal cord. These axonal connections form complex circuits that allow for the transmission of electrical signals, or action potentials, between neurons. Within these circuits, neurons communicate with one another through specialised structures called synapses, a junction between two never cells, consisting of a minute gap across which chemical neurotransmitters are released to transmit signals from one neuron to the next.

Function of Neural Pathways

Neural pathways serve as the communication highways of the brain, allowing information to be processed and transmitted rapidly and efficiently. Different pathways are responsible for different functions, such as sensory perception, motor control, emotion regulation, and higher cognitive processes. For example, the visual pathway transmits visual information from the eyes to the brain, where it is processed and interpreted to form our perception of the world around us. Similarly, the motor pathway controls voluntary movements, allowing us to walk, talk, and perform other actions.

Role in Behaviour
The structure and function of neural pathways have a profound influence on behaviour, shaping our thoughts, emotions, and actions in response to internal and external stimuli. Patterns of neural activity within specific pathways give rise to behaviours, habits, and tendencies, which can be modified and reinforced through experience and learning. For example, repeated engagement in a particular behaviour strengthens the neural pathways associated with that behaviour, making it more likely to occur in the future. Conversely, behaviours that are not reinforced weaken over time as the corresponding neural pathways are pruned through a process known as synaptic plasticity.

Plasticity and Adaptation
One of the most remarkable features of neural pathways is their ability to change and adapt in response to experience, a phenomenon known as neuroplasticity. Through processes such as synaptic strengthening, pruning, and rewiring, neural pathways can be modified to accommodate new information, learning, and environmental demands. This plasticity underlies our capacity for growth, development, and adaptation throughout life, allowing us to learn new skills,

overcome challenges, and recover from injury. Neural pathways are the building blocks of behaviour, serving as the conduits through which information flows within the brain and nervous system. By understanding the structure and function of these pathways, we gain insight into the mechanisms underlying our thoughts, emotions, and actions, and can leverage this knowledge to promote positive changes in behaviour and well-being.

15

Techniques for Strengthening Positive Neuro Pathways

Strengthening Positive Neuro Pathways

Strengthening positive neural pathways is a powerful strategy for promoting well-being, resilience, and personal growth. By intentionally engaging in activities that foster positivity and optimism, we can reshape our brains and cultivate a more positive outlook on life. In this section, we will explore several techniques for strengthening positive neural pathways and fostering a thriving mind-body connection.

Manifesting success through positive thinking involves harnessing the power of your thoughts and beliefs to create the reality you desire. Developing a positive mindset is essential for fostering resilience, well-being, and success in all aspects of life. By adopting a positive outlook and mindset, you can overcome challenges, navigate setbacks, and approach life with optimism and enthusiasm. Here are some techniques for cultivating a positive mindset:

Practice Gratitude

Gratitude is a potent tool for promoting positivity and well-being. By cultivating a daily gratitude practice, we train our brains to focus on the blessings and abundance in our lives, rather than dwelling on negativity and lack. Begin each day by reflecting on three things you're grateful for, whether it's a supportive friend, a beautiful sunset, or a delicious meal. Over time, this practice can strengthen neural pathways associated with positivity and resilience, leading to greater emotional balance and fulfilment.

Cultivate an attitude of gratitude for the blessings and opportunities in your life. Express gratitude for your achievements, as well as the challenges that have helped you grow and learn. Gratitude opens the door to abundance and attracts more positive experiences into your life.

Harness Positive Affirmations
As discussed, a few chapters back, Positive affirmations are statements that we repeat to ourselves to reinforce empowering beliefs and attitudes. By regularly affirming our worthiness, capability, and potential, we can rewire negative thought patterns and cultivate a more positive self-image. Choose affirmations that resonate with you and repeat them daily, either aloud or silently. With consistent practice, positive affirmations can strengthen neural pathways associated with self-confidence and self-esteem, empowering you to overcome challenges and pursue your goals with greater confidence and conviction. Use affirmations to reprogram your subconscious mind with positive beliefs and attitudes. Create affirmations that affirm your worth, capabilities, and potential for success. Repeat these affirmations regularly, preferably in the present tense, to reinforce your belief in yourself and your ability to achieve your goals.

Visualise Success
Visualisation is a powerful technique for strengthening positive neural pathways and manifesting your desires into reality as already discussed in chapter 8. Take a few moments

each day to visualise yourself achieving your goals and living your ideal life, imagining every detail with vivid clarity. Engage all your senses and emotions as you visualise your desired outcomes, allowing yourself to experience the joy, fulfilment, and success as if it were already happening. With regular practice, visualisation can strengthen neural pathways associated with goal achievement and increase your motivation and determination to succeed. Practice visualisation techniques to imagine yourself achieving your goals with clarity and detail. Create a mental image of your desired outcomes and immerse yourself in the experience as if it were already happening. Engage your senses and emotions to make the visualisation as vivid and real as possible, reinforcing your belief in manifesting success.

Practice Acts of Kindness
Practicing kindness and compassion towards others is not only beneficial for the recipient but also for the giver. Acts of kindness stimulate the release of feel-good hormones such as oxytocin and serotonin, which promote feelings of happiness and well-being. Engage in random acts of kindness such as helping a stranger, volunteering in your community, or expressing gratitude to someone who has made a difference in your life. These simple acts can strengthen neural pathways associated with empathy, connection, and altruism, fostering a sense of belonging and purpose.

Practice Mindfulness Meditation
Mindfulness meditation is a powerful practice for strengthening positive neural pathways and promoting emotional well-being. By bringing your attention to the present moment with openness and acceptance, mindfulness meditation can help you cultivate a greater sense of peace, clarity, and resilience in the face of life's challenges. Set aside a few minutes each day to sit quietly and focus on your breath, allowing thoughts and sensations to come and go without judgment. With regular practice, mindfulness meditation can strengthen neural pathways associated with emotional regulation and stress resilience, empowering you to navigate life's ups and downs with greater ease and equanimity.

Incorporating these techniques into your daily routine can help you strengthen positive neural pathways, promote emotional well-being, and cultivate a more positive outlook on life. We will further expand on mindfulness in two chapter yet to be discussed.

Clarify your Goals
Clearly define your goals and aspirations, both short-term and long-term. Visualise what success looks like for you and set specific, achievable objectives that align with your values and desires. Having a clear direction and purpose gives you a sense of focus and motivation to pursue your dreams. Focus on What You Want. Shift your focus from what you lack to what you want to attract into your life. Instead of dwelling on limitations and obstacles, focus your attention on opportunities, possibilities, and solutions. Directing your

thoughts towards what you want to manifest, aligns your energy with the universe and attracts positive outcomes in your life.

Stay Optimistic
Maintain a positive outlook on life, even in the face of setbacks and challenges. Trust in your ability to overcome obstacles and persevere in the pursuit of your goals. Approach difficulties with a solution-oriented mindset, focusing on what you can control and taking proactive steps towards success. Create a Positive Environment and surround yourself with positive influences, including supportive friends, mentors, and role models who uplift and inspire you. Limit your exposure to negative influences, such as pessimism, criticism, and self-doubt. Create an environment that nourishes your mind, body, and soul and fosters a sense of optimism and possibility.

Take Inspired Action
Take inspired action towards your goals, guided by intuition and inner wisdom. Trust that the universe will support you as you align your actions with your intentions and desires. Be open to opportunities and follow your intuition as you navigate the journey towards success. Eliminate Resistance and let go of resistance and attachment to specific outcomes. Release fear, doubt, and limiting beliefs that may block the flow of abundance and success into your life. Surrender control and trust in the process of manifestation. The fear for

a little vulnerability will stop you from even stepping out in the first place. And fear if permitted, will paralyse you.

Celebrate the Small Victories

Celebrate your achievements, no matter how small, and acknowledge your progress along the way. This reinforces positive thinking and motivates you to continue striving for excellence. Take time to reflect on how far you've come and express gratitude for the abundance in your life. Remember that positive thinking is a powerful tool for transformation and empowerment, and it has the potential to create profound shifts in your reality. Trust in your ability to manifest your dreams and embrace the journey with optimism, enthusiasm, and gratitude. There is very little in this life that you cannot do with a made-up mind, passion and consistency.

16

Genetics and the Environment in Transformational Thinking

Understanding the Role of Genetics and the Environment in Transformational Thinking

In exploring the complexities of transformational thinking, it is essential to understand the interplay between genetics and the environment. Both genetics and environmental factors shape our cognitive processes, behaviours, and overall potential for personal growth and change. This chapter looks into how these influences interact to affect transformational thinking, illustrated with practical examples, and tables.

The Role of Genetics

1. Genetic Predispositions
Our genetic makeup can influence various traits that are important for transformational thinking, such as cognitive abilities, temperament, and emotional regulation. Specific genes may predispose you to higher levels of creativity and or resilience.

2. Neurotransmitter Function
Genetics play a role in the production and regulation of neurotransmitters, such as dopamine, serotonin, and norepinephrine, which are crucial for motivation, mood regulation, and stress response. Variations in these genes can affect how effectively we manage stress and pursue goals.

Table: Genetic Factors Influencing Transformational Thinking

Genetic Factor	Influence on Transformational Thinking
Cognitive Abilities	Higher IQ and problem-solving skills
Temperament	Natural resilience, optimism, or emotional stability
Neurotransmitter Genes	Efficient dopamine and serotonin regulation

The Role of the Environment

1. Early Life Experiences
Early life experiences, including parenting styles, education, and socio-economic status, significantly shape our cognitive and emotional development. Positive early experiences can foster resilience, curiosity, and a growth mindset.

2. Social Interactions
The people we interact with such as our family, friends, and mentors, greatly influence our beliefs, attitudes, and behaviours. Supportive and encouraging social networks can enhance our capacity for transformational thinking.

3. Life Events and Experiences
Significant life events, whether positive or negative, can trigger profound changes in our perspectives and thinking patterns. Experiences such as travel, trauma, success, or failure contribute to our personal growth and transformation.

Table: Environmental Factors Influencing Transformational Thinking

Environmental Factor	Influence on Transformational Thinking
Early Life Experiences	Development of cognitive and emotional resilience
Social Interactions	Supportive networks enhance positive thinking
Life Events	Personal growth through significant experiences

Table: Gene-Environment Interaction Examples

Scenario	Outcome
High Intelligence Enriched Environment	Enhanced cognitive abilities and problem-solving skills
Natural Resilience Supportive Network	Increased emotional stability and growth mindset
Genetic Anxiety Stressful Environment	Heightened stress response and emotional challenges

Graph: Environmental Influence on Cognitive and Emotional Development

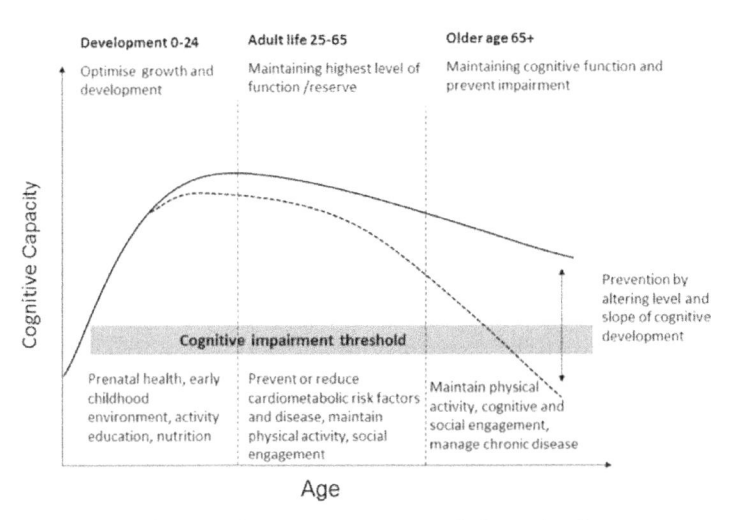

Figure 6: (Note: Source - ResearchGate.) The Interaction Between Genetics and the Environment

1. Gene-Environment Interaction

The interaction between genetic predispositions and environmental factors determines the trajectory of our cognitive and emotional development. For example, a person with a genetic predisposition for high intelligence may reach their full potential only in a stimulating environment.

2. Epigenetics
Epigenetics studies how environmental factors can influence gene expression without altering the DNA sequence. Factors such as stress, diet, and social interactions can turn genes on or off, impacting cognitive functions and behaviours.

Practical Applications

1. Personalised Growth Strategies
Understanding our genetic predispositions and environmental influences can help us develop personalised strategies for growth. For example, individuals with a genetic predisposition for anxiety can benefit from environments that provide stability and support.

2. Creating Positive Environments
We can create environments that foster transformational thinking by surrounding ourselves with positive influences, seeking out stimulating experiences, and engaging in activities that promote mental and emotional well-being.

3. Leveraging Epigenetics
By making conscious lifestyle choices such as a healthy diet, regular exercise, and stress management, we can positively influence our gene expression and overall cognitive and emotional health.

Table: Strategies for Harnessing Genetics and the Environment

Strategy	Practical Application
Personalised Growth Strategies	Tailoring learning and development plans
Creating Positive Environments	Building supportive social networks
Leveraging Epigenetics	Adopting healthy lifestyle habits

The interplay between genetics and the environment is pivotal in shaping transformational thinking. By understanding our genetic predispositions and actively creating positive environments, we can enhance our capacity for growth, resilience, and personal transformation. Embracing this knowledge empowers us to make informed choices that align with our goals and aspirations, paving the way for a fulfilling and empowered life. This chapter underscores the importance of both inherent traits and external influences in the journey of transformational thinking and harnessing mind power.

17

Change your Destiny Using your Mind

Change Your Destiny Using Your Mind

Understanding how to change your destiny using your mind involves recognising the interplay between neuroplasticity, epigenetics, brain activity, and lifestyle factors. This chapter explores how these elements interact and offers practical illustrations, tables, and graphs to elucidate these concepts. Imagine learning to play the piano. Initially, you struggle with finger placement and reading music. However, with practice, your brain strengthens the neural pathways involved in these tasks, making them easier and more automatic over time. This process is a direct result of neuroplasticity.

Epigenetics and Gene Expression

Epigenetics and Gene Expression Explained

Epigenetics involves changes in gene expression that are not caused by alterations in the DNA sequence but by external or environmental factors. These changes can affect how genes are turned on or off, influencing various physiological processes and health outcomes. Epigenetics is the study of changes in gene expression that are not caused by alterations in the underlying DNA sequence but rather by external or environmental factors. Research suggests that experiences, behaviours, and environmental influences can modulate gene expression through epigenetic mechanisms, such as DNA methylation and histone modification. While these changes do not alter the DNA sequence itself, they can affect how genes are turned on or off, potentially influencing various physiological processes and health outcomes.

Table: Epigenetic Mechanisms

Mechanism	Description
DNA Methylation	Addition of methyl groups to DNA, silencing genes
Histone Modification	Changes to proteins around which DNA is wrapped, influencing gene expression
Non-coding RNA	RNA molecules that regulate gene expression at the post-transcriptional level

Brain Activity and Gene Regulation

Influence of Brain Activity
Brain activity, including patterns of neural firing and synaptic communication, can influence gene expression within the brain. Engaging in cognitive tasks, learning new skills, and experiencing different emotional states can trigger molecular changes that modulate gene expression related to synaptic plasticity and neural connectivity. Brain activity, including patterns of neural firing and synaptic communication, can influence gene expression within the brain. For example, learning new skills, engaging in cognitive tasks, and experiencing emotional states can trigger molecular changes in neurons that modulate the expression of specific genes related to synaptic plasticity, neurotransmitter function, and

neural connectivity. These changes contribute to the brain's capacity for adaptation and learning, ultimately shaping its structure and function.

Practical Illustration: Cognitive Stimulation
Consider a scenario where an individual regularly engages in challenging puzzles or learns a new language. This cognitive stimulation leads to increased neural activity in specific brain regions, promoting gene expression changes that enhance synaptic plasticity and improve cognitive function.

Impact of Lifestyle on Gene Expression
Lifestyle factors associated with neuroplasticity, such as cognitive stimulation, physical exercise, stress management, and social engagement, can impact gene expression and contribute to overall health and well-being. While neuroplasticity itself does not directly alter DNA, lifestyle factors associated with neuroplasticity, such as cognitive stimulation, physical exercise, stress management, and social engagement, can impact gene expression and contribute to overall health and well-being. For instance, regular exercise has been shown to influence gene expression patterns related to metabolism, inflammation, and oxidative stress, leading to improved health outcomes and longevity. Similarly, mindfulness practices and stress reduction techniques may modulate gene expression associated with immune function, inflammation, and stress response.

Table: Lifestyle Factors and Gene Expression

Lifestyle Factor	Gene Expression Impact
Physical Exercise	Enhances genes related to metabolism and inflammation
Cognitive Stimulation	Promotes genes involved in neural connectivity
Stress Management	Modulates genes linked to immune function
Social Engagement	Influences genes associated with emotional regulation

Therapeutic Applications

Neuroepigenetics
Understanding the interplay between neuroplasticity and gene expression opens novel therapeutic interventions for various neurological and psychiatric disorders. By targeting epigenetic mechanisms, researchers aim to modulate neuronal function and promote neuroplasticity, offering potential treatments for conditions such as depression, anxiety, addiction, and neurodegenerative diseases.

Practical Illustration: Personalised Medicine
Imagine a future where doctors can analyse a patient's genetic and epigenetic profile to create personalised treatment plans. For instance, a person with a predisposition to depression might receive specific lifestyle recommendations and

therapies designed to promote positive gene expression changes, enhancing neuroplasticity and mental health.

While neuroplasticity does not directly alter DNA, it interacts with genetic factors and influences gene expression through epigenetic mechanisms. By understanding how brain activity and environmental influences modulate gene expression, we can harness the power of the mind to change our destiny. Embracing cognitive stimulation, physical exercise, stress management, and social engagement can lead to profound changes in our brain's structure and function, ultimately shaping a healthier, more fulfilling life. By leveraging the insights gained from neuroplasticity and epigenetics, we can create environments and adopt practices that foster our greatest potential, paving the way for personal transformation and the realisation of our aspirations.

Understanding the interplay between neuroplasticity and gene expression holds promise for developing novel therapeutic interventions for various neurological and psychiatric disorders. By targeting epigenetic mechanisms that regulate gene expression, researchers aim to modulate neuronal function and promote neuroplasticity in the context of conditions such as depression, anxiety, addiction, and neurodegenerative diseases. While still in its early stages, this emerging field of neuroepigenetics offers exciting opportunities for personalised medicine and the development of innovative treatments. While neuroplasticity itself does not directly change DNA, it can interact with genetic factors and influence gene expression through epigenetic mechanisms. With this understanding, researchers are uncovering new insights into the molecular mechanisms underlying neuroplasticity and its potential implications for health, cognition, and disease.

Change Your Destiny Using Your Mind

Changing your destiny using your mind is about harnessing the power of intentionality, mindset, and self-awareness to shape your life's path. It involves recognising the profound impact of your thoughts, beliefs, and actions on your future and taking proactive steps to align them with your highest aspirations and values. By cultivating a mindset of possibility and resilience, you can navigate the complexities of life with greater clarity and purpose, ultimately creating a destiny that reflects your true potential and essence.

The Dichotomy Between Destiny and Choice

At the heart of changing your destiny lies the intriguing dichotomy between destiny and choice. This interplay raises fundamental questions about the extent to which our lives are predetermined and the role of personal agency in shaping our future.

Destiny: The Concept of Predetermined Pathways

Destiny is often perceived as a predetermined sequence of events that unfolds according to some grand design or cosmic plan. It suggests that certain aspects of our lives are fated, and we are merely actors playing out a script written by forces beyond our control. This perspective can be comforting, offering a sense of order and purpose in the face of life's uncertainties. It implies that our experiences, relationships, and ultimate outcomes are orchestrated in a way that serves a higher purpose or contributes to a larger tapestry of existence.

Choice: The Power of Personal Agency
In contrast, the concept of choice emphasises the power of personal agency and the ability to influence our own paths through deliberate decisions and actions. It asserts that while we may be influenced by external factors and circumstances, we possess the inherent capacity to shape our lives according to our desires, values, and goals. Choice empowers us to take responsibility for our actions and to actively engage in the process of creating our reality. It is through our choices that we exercise control over our destiny, making adjustments along the way.

Navigating the Interplay
The interplay between destiny and choice can be viewed as a dynamic dance between predetermined elements and personal agency. While certain aspects of our lives may be influenced by factors beyond our control, such as genetics, early life experiences, and societal structures, we are not passive recipients of our fate. Instead, we have the power to respond to these influences with conscious intent and purposeful action.

Harnessing the Power of Choice to Shape Destiny
To harness the power of choice in shaping our destiny, it is essential to cultivate self-awareness and intentionality. Setting clear intentions helps us to focus our energy and efforts on what truly matters to us. While we exercise choice and agency, it is also important to trust the unfolding process of life. Recognising that some aspects of our journey may be beyond our immediate control can bring a sense calm as we surrender to the larger flow of life.

18

Cultivating Mindfulness

Understanding Mindfulness Meditation

Mindfulness meditation is a powerful practice that has gained widespread popularity for its profound effects on mental, emotional, and physical well-being. Rooted in ancient contemplative traditions, mindfulness meditation involves bringing focused attention to the present moment with openness, curiosity, and non-judgment. In this section, we will explore the principles and techniques of mindfulness meditation and its transformative potential for promoting self-awareness, and stress reduction.

Principles of Mindfulness
At its core, mindfulness involves paying attention to the present moment with purpose and without judgment. Rather than dwelling on the past or worrying about the future, mindfulness invites us to fully engage with our current experience, whether it's through observing our thoughts, sensations, emotions, or surroundings. By cultivating an attitude of curiosity, acceptance, and kindness towards our present-moment experience, we can cultivate greater self-awareness, emotional resilience, and inner peace.

Techniques of Mindfulness Meditation
Mindfulness meditation typically involves a formal practice in which we set aside time to sit quietly and focus our attention on a specific anchor, such as the breath, sensations in the body, or sounds in the environment. As we bring our attention to the chosen anchor, we may notice thoughts, emotions, or bodily

sensations arising. Rather than getting caught up in these distractions, we simply observe them with curiosity and non-judgment, allowing them to come and go without clinging or resistance. With regular practice, mindfulness meditation can help us develop greater clarity, concentration, and emotional regulation, leading to a deeper sense of inner peace.

Integrating Mindfulness into Daily Life
While formal meditation practice is an essential component of mindfulness, the goal is to integrate mindfulness into all aspects of daily life. Mindfulness encourages us to approach each moment with openness and curiosity, allowing us to experience life more fully and authentically. Mindfulness meditation offers a pathway to greater self-awareness, emotional resilience, and inner peace in an increasingly hectic and distracted world. Whether it's through formal meditation practice or integrating mindfulness into daily activities, mindfulness offers a powerful means of transforming our relationship to ourselves and the world, leading to greater well-being and fulfilment.

While formal mindfulness meditation practice is a valuable tool for cultivating present-moment awareness and inner peace, the true essence of mindfulness lies in its integration into all aspects of daily life. Mindfulness isn't just something we practice on the meditation cushion; it's a way of being that can profoundly transform how we experience and engage with the world around us. In this section, we will explore practical ways to integrate mindfulness into daily life and reap the benefits of greater presence, connection, and well-being.

Mindful Daily Habits
Start your day with mindfulness by incorporating mindfulness into your daily rituals, such as brushing your teeth, taking a shower, or preparing breakfast. Pay attention to the sensations, sights, sounds, and smells of each moment, bringing your full awareness to the task at hand. By approaching these activities with presence and intention, you can infuse even the most mundane tasks with a sense of meaning and joy.

Mindful Eating
Eating mindfully is a powerful way to cultivate awareness and appreciation for the nourishment that food provides. Before eating, take a moment to pause and observe the appearance, aroma, and texture of your food. As you take each bite, savour the flavours and textures, chewing slowly and mindfully. Notice any sensations in your body, such as hunger or fullness, and listen to your body's signals of hunger and satiety.

Mindful Movement
Incorporate mindfulness into your daily movement practices, such as walking, yoga, or tai chi. Pay attention to the sensations of your body as you move, noticing the rhythm of your breath, the feel of your muscles engaging, and the sensations of contact with the ground. Allow your movement to flow naturally and effortlessly, tuning into the present

moment with openness and curiosity. Mindful movement can not only enhance physical well-being but also promote mental clarity and emotional balance.

Mindful Communication
Practice mindful communication by bringing presence and awareness to your interactions with others. Listen deeply to what others are saying, without interrupting or judging, and respond with kindness and compassion. Notice any impulses to react defensively or impulsively and take a moment to pause and breathe before responding. By communicating mindfully, you can foster deeper connections with others and cultivate empathy, understanding, and mutual respect.

Mindful Work
Bring mindfulness into your workday by approaching tasks with focused attention and intention. Take regular breaks to pause and check in with yourself, noticing any tension or stress in your body, and taking steps to release it through deep breathing or gentle stretching. Practice single tasking rather than multitasking, giving your full attention to one task at a time and completing it mindfully before moving on to the next. By working mindfully, you can enhance productivity, creativity, and job satisfaction.

Integrating mindfulness into daily life is a transformative practice that can enhance every aspect of our existence, from our relationships and work to our health and well-being. By bringing presence, awareness, and intention to our daily activities, we can cultivate a deeper sense of connection to ourselves, others, and the world around us. Whether it's through mindful eating, movement, communication, or work, mindfulness offers a pathway to greater peace, fulfilment, and joy in each moment.

Box Breathing Techniques to Help with Mindfulness
Box breathing, also known as four-square breathing, is a simple yet powerful technique that can help you achieve mindfulness, reduce stress, and improve focus. This technique involves breathing in a structured pattern, typically in four equal parts, which can be visualised as a box. Here's a step-by-step guide to practicing box breathing, along with practical illustrations and graphs to help you get started.

What is Box Breathing?

Box breathing involves four steps:

Inhale: Breathe in slowly and deeply through your nose for a count of four.
Hold: Hold your breath for a count of four.
Exhale: Exhale slowly and completely through your mouth for a count of four.
Hold: Hold your breath again for a count of four.

This cycle is repeated several times to promote relaxation and mindfulness.

Benefits of Box Breathing
- Reduces stress and anxiety
- Enhances focus and concentration
- Lowers blood pressure
- Improves emotional regulation
- Promotes a sense of calm and well-being

Step-by-Step Guide to Box Breathing

Step 1: Find a Comfortable Position
Sit in a comfortable chair with your back straight and feet flat on the ground or lie down in a comfortable position.

Step 2: Visualise the Box
Imagine a box with four equal sides. Each side represents one part of the breathing cycle.

Step 3: Start the Breathing Cycle

Inhale (4 seconds) - Breathe in slowly and deeply through your nose for a count of four. Visualise moving up one side of the box.

Hold (4 seconds) - Hold your breath for a count of four. Visualise moving across the top of the box.

Exhale (4 seconds) - Exhale slowly and completely through your mouth for a count of four. Visualise moving down the other side of the box as you exhale.

Hold (4 seconds) - Hold your breath for a count of four. Visualise moving across the bottom of the box as you hold your breath.

Step 4: Repeat the Cycle
Repeat the entire cycle for several minutes, maintaining a steady, relaxed rhythm.

Diagram: Breathing Cycle
Here's a visual representation of the box breathing cycle over 16 seconds:

Phase	Duration
Inhale	4 seconds
Hold	4 seconds
Exhale	4 seconds
Hold	4 seconds

Figure 7: Diagram showing Breathing Cycle

Tips for Effective Practice
Consistency: Practice box breathing daily, even if only for a few minutes, to develop a regular habit.

Environment: Choose a quiet, comfortable place where you won't be disturbed.

Focus: Keep your focus on your breath and the visualisation of the box. If your mind wanders, gently bring it back to the practice.

Comfort: Adjust the count if needed. If four seconds feels too long, start with a count of three or even two and gradually increase as you become more comfortable.

Incorporating Box Breathing into Your Routine
Morning Routine: Start your day with a few minutes of box breathing to set a calm and focused tone.

Work Breaks: Use box breathing during breaks to reduce stress and improve concentration.

Evening Wind-Down: Incorporate box breathing into your evening routine to help unwind and prepare for sleep.

The practice of box breathing regularly, can develop mindfulness, reduce stress, and enhance your overall well-being. Remember, the key is consistency and patience, as the benefits of mindfulness and relaxation techniques build over time. To master anything in life, consistency is key. Doing it once does not solve everything, it is better to make progress in the right direction regardless of how small the progress.

19

The Benefits of Mindful Practice

The Benefits of Mindfulness Practice

In this section, we will explore the myriad benefits of mindfulness practice and its transformative potential for enhancing every aspect of our lives. Numerous studies have demonstrated the myriad benefits of mindfulness meditation for mental, emotional, and physical health. Research suggests that regular practice of mindfulness meditation can reduce symptoms of stress, anxiety, depression, and chronic pain, while improving cognitive function, immune function, and overall quality of life.

Mindfulness meditation involves focusing on the present moment without judgment. It helps you become aware of your thoughts, emotions, and bodily sensations. Self-awareness, the ability to recognise and understand one's own thoughts, emotions, and behaviours, is a cornerstone of personal growth and fulfilment. Cultivating self-awareness allows us to live more consciously, make more informed decisions, and navigate life's challenges with greater clarity and resilience. In this section, we will explore several techniques for enhancing self-awareness and deepening our understanding of ourselves.

Mindfulness meditation is a powerful practice for developing self-awareness by bringing focused attention to the present moment with openness and curiosity. Through regular meditation practice, we learn to observe our thoughts, emotions, and bodily sensations without judgment or attachment, gaining insight into the inner workings of our minds. By cultivating mindfulness, we develop greater clarity, insight, and self-acceptance, enabling us to respond to life's challenges with greater wisdom and equanimity.

Illustration: Mindfulness Meditation Process

1. Find a Quiet Space: Sit comfortably in a quiet environment.
2. Focus on Breath: Pay attention to your breathing.
3. Observe Thoughts: Notice any thoughts or feelings that arise.
4. Return to Breath: Gently bring your focus back to your breath.
5. Repeat: Continue for 5-10 minutes.

Mindfulness and Mental Health

Numerous studies have demonstrated the extensive benefits of mindfulness meditation for mental, emotional, and physical health. Research suggests that regular practice of mindfulness meditation can reduce symptoms of stress, anxiety, depression, and chronic pain while improving cognitive function, immune function, and overall wellbeing.

Stress Reduction

One of the most well-documented benefits of mindfulness practice is its ability to reduce stress and promote relaxation. By cultivating present-moment awareness and non-judgmental acceptance, mindfulness helps us step out of the cycle of rumination and worry that often accompanies stress, allowing us to respond to challenges with greater clarity and equanimity. Regular mindfulness practice has been shown to lower levels of stress hormones such as cortisol, leading to improved resilience and overall well-being.

Improved Emotional Regulation
Mindfulness practice can enhance our ability to recognise, understand, and regulate our emotions effectively. By observing our thoughts, feelings, and bodily sensations with curiosity and compassion, we develop greater emotional intelligence and resilience. Mindfulness allows us to create space between stimulus and response, enabling us to choose how we react to challenging situations rather than reacting impulsively or habitually. This increased emotional regulation can lead to greater inner peace, stability, and harmony in our relationships and daily interactions.

Cognitive Enhancements Through Mindfulness
Enhanced Cognitive Function
Numerous studies have demonstrated the cognitive benefits of mindfulness practice, including improved attention, concentration, and memory. By training our minds to focus on the present moment without distraction, mindfulness enhances our capacity to sustain attention and filter out irrelevant information. This heightened cognitive function can lead to improved performance in academic, professional, and creative endeavours, as well as greater mental clarity and problem-solving skills.

Greater Self-Awareness
Mindfulness practice fosters a deep sense of self-awareness by inviting us to explore the inner workings of our minds with curiosity and non-judgment. Through mindful observation of our thoughts, emotions, and sensations, we gain insight into our habitual patterns, reactions, and tendencies, allowing us to break free from unconscious conditioning and make more conscious choices in our lives. This increased self-awareness can lead to greater authenticity and self-acceptance.

Mindfulness and Overall Well-Being
Enhanced Well-being and Resilience
Mindfulness practice has been linked to greater overall well-being and resilience in the face of life's challenges. By cultivating present-moment awareness and acceptance, mindfulness helps us develop a more balanced and compassionate perspective on ourselves and the world around us. This sense of inner peace and equanimity enables us to navigate life's ups and downs with greater grace, courage, and resilience, leading to deeper satisfaction.

Integrating Mindfulness into Daily Life
The benefits of mindfulness practice are vast and far-reaching, encompassing improvements in physical health, emotional well-being, cognitive function, and interpersonal relationships. By integrating mindfulness into our daily lives through formal meditation practice and informal mindfulness exercises, we can unlock our full potential for

growth, healing, and transformation. Mindfulness offers a pathway to greater peace, clarity, and authenticity, empowering us to live more fully and joyfully in each moment. Whether through a structured practice like meditation or simply bringing mindful awareness to everyday activities, the consistent application of mindfulness can lead to profound changes in how we experience and engage with the world around us.

Mindfulness practice provides a powerful tool for enhancing well-being and fostering personal growth. By embracing the principles of mindfulness and integrating them into our daily routines, we can transform our relationship with ourselves, others, and the world at large. The journey of mindfulness is one of continuous discovery and enrichment, offering endless opportunities for cultivating a more peaceful, present, and fulfilling life. The benefits of mindfulness practice are vast and far-reaching, encompassing improvements in physical health, emotional well-being, cognitive function, and interpersonal relationships. Mindfulness offers a pathway to greater peace, clarity, and authenticity, empowering us to live more fully in each moment.

20

Developing Self-Awareness

The Importance of Self-Reflection

Self-reflection is a profound practice that invites us to turn our attention inward and explore the depths of our thoughts, emotions, and experiences. In a world filled with constant noise and distraction, self-reflection provides a sacred space for introspection, insight, and personal growth. In this chapter, we will look into the importance of self-reflection and its transformative potential for fostering self-awareness, resilience, and authenticity.

Cultivating Self-Awareness
Self-reflection is a powerful tool for cultivating self-awareness – the ability to recognise and understand our thoughts, emotions, and behaviours. Take time to pause and reflect on your experiences, and you will gain insight into your own beliefs, values, and motivations, allowing you to make more conscious choices that affect your everyday life.

Practical Illustration:
Journaling for Self-Awareness
Start a daily journaling practice. Each evening, take 10-15 minutes to write about your day. Reflect on the following prompts:

- What emotions did I experience today, and what triggered them?
- How did my actions align with my core values?
- What patterns in my behaviour do I notice?

Regular journaling creates a habit of introspection, making it easier to recognise personal patterns and gain deeper self-awareness.

Nurturing Emotional Intelligence
Self-reflection plays a crucial role in nurturing emotional intelligence, which is the ability to recognise, understand, and manage our own emotions, as well as the emotions of others. Through self-reflection, we develop greater empathy, compassion, and self-regulation, enhancing our ability to successfully navigate interpersonal relationships with grace and wisdom.

Practical Illustration: Reflective Pause Technique
Whenever you experience a strong emotion, take a reflective pause:

1. **Stop and breathe:** Take three deep breaths to center yourself.
2. **Observe:** Notice the emotion without judgment. Ask yourself, "What am I feeling right now?"
3. **Reflect:** Consider what triggered this emotion and why. What does this emotion tell you about your needs or values?
4. **Respond:** Choose a mindful response that aligns with your values and the situation.

Practical Illustration: Meditation for Insight
Incorporate a 10-minute daily meditation practice focused on self-reflection:

1. Find a quiet space and sit comfortably.
2. Close your eyes and take a few deep breaths to relax.
3. Focus your attention on your breath or a specific question about your life.
4. After your meditation, write down any insights or thoughts that arose.

Self-reflection enhances our ability to make informed and intentional decisions that align with our values and aspirations. Regularly practicing this technique helps build emotional resilience and better manage reactions.

Decision Reflection Exercise
After making a significant decision, set aside time to reflect on the process and outcome:

- What were the key factors that influenced my decision?
- How do I feel about the outcome?
- What did I learn from this experience?

Regularly conducting this exercise sharpens your decision-making skills and ensures your choices are aligned with your long-term goals.

Fostering Resilience and Well-Being
Self-reflection is a vital tool for fostering resilience and well-being in the face of life's inevitable challenges and setbacks. By developing a practice of self-compassion and self-care, we develop the inner resources necessary to weather the inevitable storms of life with grace and resilience.

Practical Illustration: Self-Compassion Break
When facing a difficult situation, take a self-compassion break:

1. **Acknowledge:** Recognise that you are experiencing a moment of suffering.
2. **Soothe:** Place your hand over your heart and take a few deep breaths.
3. **Affirm:** Repeat a compassionate phrase, such as "May I be kind to myself in this moment."

Incorporating self-compassion breaks into your routine helps build resilience and promotes overall well-being. Self-reflection is a fundamental practice for cultivating self-awareness, nurturing emotional intelligence, facilitating personal growth, enhancing decision-making skills, and fostering resilience and well-being. Practicing exercises like journaling, meditation, and reflective pauses can make self-reflection a regular and impactful part of your daily life. These practices not only enhance your personal growth but also help you build stronger relationships, make better decisions, and maintain emotional balance.

21

Techniques for Enhancing Self-awareness

Overview

In our fast-paced, modern world, the quest for self-awareness is more crucial than ever. Self-awareness is the cornerstone of personal development, influencing how we perceive ourselves, interact with others, and navigate the complexities of life. It involves a deep understanding of our thoughts, emotions, motivations, and behaviours, enabling us to live more consciously and authentically. This chapter looks into a range of techniques designed to enhance self-awareness. Whether you are embarking on a journey of self-discovery for the first time or seeking to deepen your existing self-awareness, these techniques will provide practical tools to foster greater clarity, emotional intelligence, and personal growth.

We will explore methods such as mindfulness meditation, reflective journaling, and feedback-seeking, each offering unique pathways to self-understanding. Additionally, we will examine the role of self-compassion in self-awareness, highlighting how a kind and non-judgmental attitude towards oneself can facilitate deeper introspection and acceptance. By the end of this chapter, you will be equipped with a diverse toolkit of self-awareness techniques, empowering you to embark on a transformative journey of inner exploration.

1. Journaling

Technique Overview

Journaling involves writing down your thoughts, feelings, and reflections. It helps in processing emotions and gaining insight into your behaviour and the way your mind is set.

Illustration: Journaling Structure
1. **Date and Time:** Start with the current date and time.
2. **Prompt or Question**: Write a prompt or question to focus on (e.g., "What am I grateful for today?").
3. **Free Write:** Write freely about your thoughts and feelings related to the prompt.
4. **Reflection:** Reflect on what you've written and note any insights or patterns.

Table: Journaling Prompts and Their Benefits

Prompt	Purpose	Benefits
What am I grateful for?	Cultivate gratitude	Boosts positivity and happiness
How did I handle stress today?	Analyse stress responses	Identifies stressors and coping strategies
What are my current goals?	Clarify objectives	Enhances focus and motivation

2. Self-Reflection

Technique Overview

Self-reflection involves examining your own thoughts and behaviours to gain deeper insights into your actions and motivations. Engaging in self-reflection exercises can help enhance self-awareness by prompting us to examine our thoughts, emotions, and behaviours more closely. For example, we can ask ourselves reflective questions such as "What am I feeling right now?" or "What are my core values and beliefs?" These exercises encourage us to pause and explore our inner experience with curiosity and openness, fostering greater self-awareness.

Illustration: Self-Reflection Process
1. Set Aside Time: Allocate a specific time for reflection (e.g., end of day).
2. Ask Questions: Use questions to guide your reflection (e.g., "What went well today?").
3. Write Down Insights: Record your observations and insights.
4. Identify Patterns: Look for recurring themes or patterns in your reflections.
5. Set Goals: Based on your insights, set goals for improvement.

3. Emotional Check-Ins

Technique Overview
Emotional check-ins involve periodically assessing and acknowledging your emotional state throughout the day. Emotional check-ins are a valuable practice for enhancing self-awareness by regularly assessing and acknowledging your emotional state throughout the day. This technique involves pausing at designated times to reflect on how you're feeling, identifying the specific emotions you're experiencing, and rating their intensity. By systematically recording these feelings and noting any patterns or triggers, emotional check-ins help you gain deeper insights into your

emotional landscape. This practice not only fosters greater emotional intelligence but also empowers you to respond more effectively to your emotional needs and manage stress more proactively. Through consistent use of emotional check-ins, you can cultivate a more nuanced understanding of your inner world, leading to improved self-regulation.

Illustration: Emotional Check-In Process

1. Set Reminders: Schedule regular reminders (e.g., every 2 hours).
2. Pause and Assess: Take a moment to check in with yourself.
3. Identify Emotion: Note the emotion you're feeling (e.g., happy, stressed, anxious).
4. Rate Intensity: Rate the intensity of the emotion on a scale of 1-10.
5. Record and Reflect: Record your findings and reflect on any patterns or triggers.

Table: Emotional Check-In Scale

Emotion	Rating (1-10)	Notes
Happy	7	Felt good after completing a project.
Stressed	5	Stress due to a tight deadline.
Anxious	3	Anxiety about an upcoming presentation.

4. Feedback from Others

Technique Overview
Seeking feedback from others involves asking for their perspectives on your behaviour, actions, and interpersonal skills. Seeking feedback from others and reflecting on it can be a powerful way to enhance self-awareness. By soliciting feedback from trusted friends, mentors, or colleagues, we gain valuable insights into how others perceive us and our behaviour. Reflecting on this feedback with openness and humility allows us to gain a deeper understanding of ourselves and how we impact those around us. By integrating feedback into our self-awareness practice, we can identify areas for growth and development and cultivate greater self-awareness.

Illustration: Seeking and Utilising Feedback
1. Identify Feedback Sources: Choose individuals who know you well (e.g., colleagues, friends).
2. Ask Specific Questions: Request feedback on specific areas (e.g., teamwork).
3. Receive Feedback Openly: Listen without becoming defensive.
4. Reflect on Feedback: Consider the feedback and how it aligns with your self-perception.
5. Implement Changes: Adjust based on the feedback received.

22

Obstacles to Self-Understanding

Overcoming Obstacles to Self-Understanding

Self-understanding, the ability to know oneself deeply and authentically, is a fundamental aspect of personal growth and fulfilment. However, the journey toward self-understanding is not always easy and can be fraught with obstacles and challenges. In this section, we will explore common obstacles to self-understanding and strategies for overcoming them, allowing us to deepen our understanding of ourselves and live more authentically.

Fear of Self-Exploration
Fear can be a significant obstacle to self-understanding, as it may prevent us from delving deep into our thoughts, emotions, and experiences. Fear of confronting painful truths or acknowledging our vulnerabilities can lead us to avoid self-exploration altogether, keeping us stuck in patterns of denial or avoidance. To overcome this obstacle, it's essential to cultivate courage and compassion toward us. By gently confronting our fears with kindness and curiosity, we can create a safe space for self-exploration and begin to unravel the layers of our innermost selves.

Negative Self-Talk
Negative self-talk, or the inner critic, can undermine our efforts to understand ourselves by distorting our perceptions and reinforcing limiting beliefs. The constant stream of self-critical thoughts can create a barrier between us and our true selves, obscuring our innate worthiness and potential. To

overcome this obstacle, it's crucial to cultivate self-compassion and self-awareness. By recognising and challenging our negative self-talk with kindness and understanding, we can cultivate a more balanced and compassionate relationship with ourselves, allowing us to see ourselves more clearly and authentically.

Unconscious Biases and Blind Spots
Unconscious biases and blind spots can hinder our ability to understand ourselves fully, as they may prevent us from seeing aspects of ourselves that lie outside our awareness. These biases and blind spots are often shaped by past experiences, cultural conditioning, and social influences, leading us to perceive ourselves in narrow or distorted ways. To overcome this obstacle, it's essential to cultivate mindfulness and self-reflection. Adding conscious awareness to our thoughts, emotions, and behaviours, helps us uncover and challenge unconscious biases and blind spots, allowing us to see ourselves more clearly and authentically.

External Expectations and Social Comparisons
External expectations and social comparisons can create pressure to conform to societal norms or others' expectations, leading us to adopt identities or behaviours that are not aligned with our true selves. This can result in feelings of disconnection, confusion, or inauthenticity, making it difficult to understand ourselves fully. To overcome this obstacle, it's essential to cultivate self-awareness and self-acceptance. By tuning into our innermost desires, values, and

aspirations, we can begin to discern our authentic selves from external influences, allowing us to live in alignment with our true nature and purpose.

Resistance to Change
Resistance to change can be a significant obstacle to self-understanding, as it may prevent us from embracing growth opportunities or exploring new aspects of ourselves. Fear of the unknown or discomfort with uncertainty can keep us stuck in familiar patterns, inhibiting our ability to evolve and grow. To overcome this obstacle, it's essential to cultivate openness and curiosity toward us. Embracing change as a natural and inevitable part of the human experience, will create space for self-discovery and transformation, allowing us to deepen our understanding of ourselves. Overcoming obstacles to self-understanding requires courage, compassion, and commitment to the journey of self-discovery and will lead to embracing our authentic selves, and change. This will unlock the door to greater clarity and authenticity in our lives.

23

Developing Emotional Intelligence

Developing Emotional Intelligence

Emotional intelligence (EI) is a transformative skill that significantly influences our ability to navigate the complexities of life and relationships. Unlike traditional measures of intelligence, which focus on cognitive abilities such as logic and reasoning, emotional intelligence encompasses a broader range of competencies that govern how we perceive, understand, and manage our own emotions and the emotions of others. These skills are crucial for fostering healthy relationships, making informed decisions, and achieving both personal and professional success.

In today's interconnected world, where collaboration and communication are key, the importance of emotional intelligence cannot be overstated. High EI allows us to handle interpersonal dynamics with finesse, resolve conflicts effectively, and build strong, empathetic connections with others. It also plays a pivotal role in leadership, where understanding and managing emotions can inspire and motivate teams, leading to a more cohesive and productive work environment. In this chapter we look into the fundamental components of emotional intelligence: self-awareness, self-regulation, motivation, empathy, and social skills. Each of these elements contributes to a well-rounded emotional intelligence profile and enhancing them can lead to profound improvements in how we interact with the world around us.

Emotional Intelligence Components and Development Strategies

Component	Description	Development Strategies
Self-Awareness	Recognising and understanding your own emotions	Emotional check-ins, mindfulness practices, journaling
Self-Regulation	Managing your emotions effectively	Deep breathing exercises, stress management techniques, meditation
Motivation	Using emotions to pursue goals	Goal setting, positive affirmations, self-reflection
Empathy	Understanding and sharing the feelings of others	Active listening, perspective-taking exercises, compassion training
Social Skills	Managing relationships to move people in desired directions	Communication skills training, conflict resolution strategies

Table: Daily Emotional Check-In

Day	Time	Emotion	Intensity (1-10)	Trigger/Event
Monday	9 am	Anxious	7	Meeting with boss
Monday	3 pm	Calm	4	Completed project task
Tuesday	11 am	Frustrated	6	Traffic jam
Tuesday	6 pm	Happy	8	Dinner with family
Wednesday	10 am	Focused	5	Working on a new project

Developing Empathy: Active Listening Exercise

Exercise Description:

Step 1: Pair up with a partner.
Step 2: One person speaks about a recent experience.
Step 3: The listener paraphrases and reflects what they heard.
Step 4: Switch roles and repeat.

Empathy Development Progress:

Week	Active Listening Sessions	Empathy Score (1-10)
1	3	5
2	3	6
3	4	7
4	4	8

Understanding Emotional Intelligence (EI)
Emotional Intelligence (EI) is a critical skill that shapes how we perceive, understand, and manage our emotions and the emotions of others. It encompasses a range of abilities, including self-awareness, self-regulation, empathy, social skills, and motivation. These skills are essential for navigating the complexities of human relationships and achieving personal and professional success. In this chapter, we will explore the components of emotional intelligence and its profound impact on various aspects of our lives.

Self-Awareness and Self-Regulation Skills

Self-Awareness
Start by cultivating self-awareness, the cornerstone of emotional intelligence. This involves a deep understanding of your own emotions, strengths, weaknesses, and triggers. Here are some detailed strategies:

- **Mindfulness Practices**: Engage in mindfulness techniques such as meditation and self-reflection. These practices help you observe your thoughts, emotions, and physical sensations without judgment. For example, dedicate a few minutes each day to mindful breathing or a body scan to stay grounded in the present moment.
- **Journaling**: Keep a journal to track your emotional patterns and triggers. Write about your daily experiences, noting any significant emotional reactions and the circumstances that triggered them. Reflect on

these entries regularly to identify recurring themes and insights.

- **Feedback from Others**: Seek feedback from trusted friends, family, or colleagues to gain an external perspective on your behaviour and emotional responses. This can provide valuable insights that you might overlook on your own.

Self-Regulation

Learn to regulate your emotions by developing self-regulation skills. These skills help you manage stress, anxiety, and impulsive reactions effectively. These include:

- **Deep Breathing**: Practice deep breathing exercises to calm your nervous system. For instance, try the 4-7-8 technique: inhale for 4 seconds, hold your breath for 7 seconds, and exhale for 8 seconds.

- **Progressive Muscle Relaxation**: This involves tensing and then relaxing different muscle groups in your body, which can help reduce physical tension and promote relaxation.

- **Visualisation**: Use visualisation techniques to create calming mental images. Picture yourself in a peaceful place or visualise a positive outcome to a stressful situation.

- **Cognitive Reappraisal**: Reframe negative thoughts and emotions in a more positive light. For example, instead of thinking, "I failed because I'm not good enough," reframe it as, "This is a learning opportunity, and I can improve with practice."

Empathy and Social Skills

Empathy
Empathy involves understanding and sharing the feelings of others. Enhancing empathy can significantly improve your relationships and social interactions:

- **Active Listening**: Focus on truly listening to others without interrupting. Show interest by nodding, maintaining eye contact, and asking clarifying questions. This demonstrates that you value their perspective and are fully engaged.

- **Perspective-Taking**: Practice putting yourself in others' shoes to understand their emotions and viewpoints. For example, if a colleague is frustrated, consider what might be causing their frustration and how you would feel in their situation.

- **Nonverbal Cues**: Pay attention to body language, facial expressions, and tone of voice. These nonverbal signals can provide important clues about how someone is feeling.

Social Skills

Developing strong social skills helps you navigate interpersonal interactions more effectively:

- **Active Listening**: Beyond empathy, active listening involves giving others your full attention, avoiding distractions, and reflecting back what you've heard to ensure understanding.

- **Assertiveness**: Express your needs and boundaries clearly and respectfully. For instance, if you need more time to complete a task, communicate this directly and constructively.

- **Conflict Resolution**: Learn techniques for resolving disagreements constructively. This includes negotiation, finding common ground, and being willing to compromise.

Motivation

Cultivating Intrinsic Motivation

Intrinsic motivation is driven by internal rewards and personal satisfaction rather than external incentives. To cultivate it:

- **Align Goals with Values and Passions**: Reflect on your core values and passions and set goals that resonate with them. For example, if you value helping others, set goals related to volunteer work or mentoring.

- **Set Meaningful Goals**: Ensure your goals are specific, measurable, achievable, relevant, and time-bound (SMART). Break them down into manageable steps to maintain momentum and focus. For instance, if your goal is to write a book, break it down into smaller tasks like outlining and or writing a chapter a month.

- **Self-Discipline and Perseverance**: Develop routines that support your goals, such as dedicating specific times each day to work on them. Stay committed even when faced with setbacks by reminding yourself of the deeper purpose behind your efforts.

- **Celebrate Successes and Learn from Failures**: Acknowledge and reward yourself for achieving milestones, no matter how small. Reflect on failures as learning opportunities, analysing what went wrong and how you can improve next time.

Increasing Awareness and Challenging Assumptions

Understanding Unconscious Biases
To address unconscious biases:

- **Educate Yourself**: Learn about common biases, such as racial, gender, and age biases. Reflect on how these might influence your thoughts, attitudes, and behaviours.

- **Reflect on Assumptions**: Pay attention to moments when you make snap judgments based on stereotypes. Challenge these assumptions by questioning their validity and seeking diverse perspectives.

- **Engage with Diverse Groups**: Actively engage with people from different backgrounds and cultures. Listen to their stories to broaden your understanding and challenge implicit biases.

Interrupting Biased Thinking

- **Pause and Reflect**: When you notice biased thoughts, take a moment to assess their accuracy and fairness. Consider alternative perspectives and actively reframe your thinking.

- **Bias Mitigation Strategies**: Implement strategies like structured decision-making processes, blind evaluations, and diversity training programs to reduce bias. Encourage accountability and transparency in decision-making to promote fairness.

Seeking Feedback and Support

- **Solicit Feedback**: Ask for feedback from others about your behaviour and interactions. This can help you identify and address biases and improve your emotional intelligence.

- **Professional Guidance**: Consider working with a therapist, coach, or mentor for personalised support and strategies. They can provide insights and accountability as you work on developing your EI.

Commit to Continuous Learning

- **Stay Informed**: Keep up with the latest research and best practices related to unconscious bias, diversity, equity, and inclusion.

- **Self-Reflection**: Engage in ongoing self-reflection to challenge biases and foster an inclusive mindset.

- **Create Inclusive Environments**: Promote fairness, equity, and inclusion in all areas of your life by actively addressing biases and creating environments where everyone feels valued and respected. Emotional intelligence offers a pathway to deeper self-understanding, richer relationships, and greater resilience, empowering you to thrive in all areas of life.

24

Slip of the tongue

Slip of the Tongue:

Unravelling the Mysteries of Verbal Missteps
Imagine speaking in a crucial meeting or during an intimate conversation, and suddenly, you blurt out a word or phrase you never intended to say. This phenomenon, known as a "slip of the tongue," is a common and often amusing occurrence where our words betray our true intentions, revealing the intricate and sometimes precarious nature of language processing in the human brain. While these verbal slips are usually minor and easily corrected, they provide a window into the subconscious mind and the complex mechanisms that govern our speech.

In this chapter, we will explore the fascinating world of slips of the tongue, exploring their causes, types, and implications. We will examine the psychological and neurological underpinnings of these linguistic errors and consider what they reveal about the inner workings of our minds. From the Freudian slip that hints at hidden desires to the simple spoonerism that provokes laughter, these verbal mishaps are more than mere accidents, they are clues to the sophisticated and often mysterious processes that enable us to communicate. Through this exploration, the aim is to enhance our understanding of language, cognition, and the human condition itself.

Understanding Slips of the Tongue

Slips of the tongue occur when the brain processes language too quickly, leading to errors in speech production. These errors can result in the substitution, omission, or rearrangement of words or sounds. This chapter looks into the various forms these slips can take, their underlying causes, and what they reveal about our cognitive processes.

Types of Slips of the Tongue

1. **Phonemic Errors**

- **Definition**: These involve substituting one sound or phoneme for another, resulting in words that sound similar but have different meanings.
- **Example**: Saying "television" instead of "telephone."
- **Practical Example**: You're on a phone call with a friend and mean to ask, "Can you hand me the telephone?" but instead, you say, "Can you hand me the television?" Both words start with 'tele' and your brain mixes them up.

2. **Semantic Errors**

- **Definition**: These involve substituting one word for another with a similar meaning.
- **Example**: Saying "cat" instead of "dog."
- **Practical Example:** While talking about pets, you mean to say, "I need to walk my dog," but you

accidentally say, "I need to walk my cat," causing a moment of confusion.

3. **Morphological Errors**

- **Definition**: These involve errors in word structure, such as adding or omitting affixes.
- **Example**: Saying "runned" instead of "ran."
- **Practical Example**: During a conversation, you say, "He runned fast," instead of "He ran fast." The incorrect use of the past tense form highlights a common morphological slip.

4. **Blends**

- **Definition**: These involve combining two words or phrases, often resulting in a nonsensical or humorous utterance.
- **Example**: Saying "smog" instead of "smoke" and "fog."
- **Practical Example**: You're describing the weather and mean to say, "It's a mix of smoke and fog," but instead, you say, "It's smoggy today," blending the two words into one.

Causes of Slips of the Tongue

Slips of the tongue can occur due to various factors, including:

- **Cognitive Processing Limitations:** The brain processes language at high speed, and sometimes this rapid processing leads to errors.
- **Distraction:** When your attention is divided, you're more likely to make speech errors.
- **Fatigue:** Being tired can impair cognitive function, leading to more frequent slips.
- **Linguistic Interference:** Bilingual or multilingual speakers may mix elements from different languages, leading to slips.

Revealing the Subconscious: Freudian Slips

In some cases, slips of the tongue can reveal underlying thoughts, feelings, or intentions that the speaker may not consciously be aware of, often referred to as Freudian slips. For instance, a person might accidentally call their partner by an ex's name, possibly indicating unresolved feelings. However, it's crucial to interpret such instances with caution, as they can also be purely accidental and unrelated to subconscious desires.

Practical Examples of Slips of the Tongue

1. **Workplace Scenario:**
   - **Situation**: During a meeting, you're discussing quarterly goals and accidentally say, "We need to increase our garbage," instead of "increase our margins."

- **Explanation**: This phonemic error might occur due to the similar ending sounds in "margins" and "garbage." Such errors can lead to brief moments of embarrassment but are typically understood and corrected quickly.

2. **Family Dinner:**
- **Situation**: While setting the table, you mean to ask someone to "pass the pepper," but you say, "pass the pepper," combining "pass the salt" and "pass the pepper."
- **Explanation**: This blend error illustrates how common phrases can get mixed up, leading to humorous situations.

3. **Public Speaking:**
- **Situation**: Giving a speech, you intend to say, "Our future is bright," but you accidentally say, "Our future is fight."
- **Explanation**: This slip could be due to nervousness or cognitive processing speed, where similar-sounding words are easily confused.

The Transformative Power of Recognising Slips
Understanding slips of the tongue can enhance our self-awareness and improve our communication skills. By recognising the factors that lead to these errors, we can become more mindful speakers. Here are some practical tips:

- **Mindfulness Practice**: Engaging in mindfulness can help you stay present and focused, reducing the likelihood of distraction-related slips.
- **Adequate Rest**: Ensuring you get enough rest can help maintain cognitive function and reduce fatigue-related errors.
- **Language Exercises**: Practicing language exercises, especially for multilingual individuals, can help mitigate linguistic interference.

Slips of the tongue are a natural aspect of language production, reflecting the complexities of our cognitive processes. While they can lead to amusing or embarrassing moments, they are usually harmless and quickly corrected. Understanding the different types of slips, their causes, and practical ways to manage them, can improve your communication and gain insights into the workings of your mind. Embracing these moments with humour and curiosity can transform how you view your verbal missteps, making them a valuable part of your personal growth and self-awareness journey.

25

Breaking Bad Habits

Breaking Bad *Habits*

Identifying and understanding habits is essential for taking control of your subconscious mind and making positive changes in your life. Habits are automatic behaviours that we perform regularly, often without conscious thought. They are formed through repetition and reinforcement and can have a significant impact on our daily routines, productivity, and overall well-being. Here's how you can identify and understand your habits in greater detail:

Observation
Start by observing your daily routines and behaviours with curiosity and non-judgment. Notice recurring patterns in your actions, such as what you do upon waking up, how you spend your free time, and how you respond to certain triggers or situations.

Example: Each morning, do you automatically reach for your phone to check social media? Observe this action without judging yourself. Simply note when it happens and how it makes you feel.

Keep a Habit Journal
Keep a journal or log of your daily habits and routines. Record details such as the time of day, the behaviour performed, the trigger or cue that preceded it, and any thoughts or emotions associated with the habit. This can help you identify patterns and gain insights into your habits.

Example: Write down every time you feel the urge to snack. Note what you were doing right before the urge hit (e.g., watching TV, feeling stressed), what you ate, and how you felt afterward.

Identify Triggers

Pay attention to the triggers or cues that prompt your habits. Triggers can be external stimuli, such as time of day, location, or social cues, or internal cues, such as emotions, thoughts, or bodily sensations. Understanding your triggers can help you anticipate and modify your habits more effectively.

Example: If you tend to procrastinate when you feel overwhelmed, recognise the feeling of being overwhelmed as a trigger. Notice what happens right before you start procrastinating, like checking emails instead of working.

Examine Rewards

Consider the rewards or outcomes that reinforce your habits. Habits are often maintained because they provide some form of gratification or reward, whether physical, emotional, or psychological. Reflect on what you gain from each habit and whether the rewards align with your values and goals.

Example: If you eat junk food when stressed, the immediate reward might be comfort and a temporary relief from stress. However, consider if this aligns with your long-term health goals. Are there healthier rewards that can provide similar comfort?

Recognise Habit Loops

Habits typically follow a three-step loop: cue, routine, and reward. The cue triggers the habit, the routine is the behaviour itself, and the reward is the positive reinforcement that reinforces the habit. By recognising this loop, you can identify opportunities to intervene and modify your habits.

Example:
- **Cue:** Feeling tired in the afternoon.
- **Routine:** Drinking coffee.
- **Reward:** Feeling more alert. Consider replacing the coffee with a quick walk to see if the new routine provides the same reward and feeling.

Assess Habit Patterns

Look for patterns or clusters of habits that tend to occur together or in specific contexts. For example, you may notice that you engage in certain habits when feeling stressed or bored, or that certain environments or social settings trigger particular behaviours. Understanding these patterns can help you address multiple habits simultaneously.

Example: You might find that you overeat and binge-watch TV shows when you are alone at home in the evenings. Recognising this pattern allows you to create a plan to address both habits together, perhaps by scheduling evening activities with friends or engaging in a hobby.

Reflect on Habit Consequences
Consider the long-term consequences of your habits on your health, well-being, relationships, and goals. Some habits may contribute to your growth and success, while others may be detrimental or counterproductive. Reflect on whether your habits align with your values and aspirations and whether they support your overall well-being.

Example: Regular exercise may lead to improved health and energy levels, while excessive screen time could lead to eye strain and reduced productivity. Reflect on whether your habits are helping or hindering your progress.

Practical Steps for Identifying and Understanding Habits

1. **Daily Review:** Set aside a few minutes each day to reflect on your actions and note any recurring behaviours.

    Example: Each night, jot down key habits you noticed throughout the day in your journal.

2. **Weekly Analysis**: At the end of each week, review your habit journal to identify common triggers and rewards.

    Example: Notice if stress at work consistently leads to late-night snacking.

3. **Set Intentions**: For each habit you identify, set a clear intention to either maintain, modify, or eliminate it.

   Example: If you find you procrastinate by browsing social media, set a goal to limit social media use during work hours.

4. **Mindfulness Practice**: Incorporate mindfulness techniques to become more aware of your thoughts and actions.

   Example: Practice deep breathing or meditation to center yourself and reduce impulsive habits.

5. **Positive Reinforcement:** Reinforce new, positive habits with rewards that align with your values.

   Example: Treat yourself to a small reward after completing a productive work session, like a short walk or a favourite snack.

Taking the time to identify and understand your habits, will help you gain valuable insights into your subconscious programming and make informed decisions about which habits to maintain, modify, or eliminate. With awareness and intentionality, you can harness the power of your subconscious mind to cultivate positive habits that align with your goals and lead to lasting personal transformation.

26

Strategies for Breaking Negative Patterns

Breaking Negative Habits

Transforming Your Life for the Better
We all have habits. We all have routines and behaviours that we perform almost automatically. While some habits are beneficial, others can be detrimental to our well-being, productivity, and happiness. Breaking negative habits is a challenging yet essential process for anyone striving to improve their life. It involves understanding the underlying triggers, identifying healthier replacement behaviours, and consistently applying new strategies to replace unwanted habits. In this chapter, we will embark on a comprehensive journey to break free from negative habits and transform them into positive, life-enhancing routines. We'll explore the psychology behind habit formation, explore the factors that perpetuate negative behaviours, and provide practical, illustrated guides to help you implement effective strategies for change. Understanding the science of habits and applying evidence-based techniques will help you overcome the inertia of negative patterns and cultivate a purposeful life.

Our exploration will include:

1. **Understanding Habit Formation**: Learn about the habit loop, consisting of cue, routine, and reward, and how this cycle sustains both positive and negative habits.

2. **Identifying Triggers**: Discover the importance of recognising the environmental, emotional, and situational triggers that initiate negative habits, and how to address them effectively.

3. **Replacement Behaviours**: Explore strategies for identifying and adopting healthier behaviours that can take the place of negative habits, ensuring a smoother transition and sustained change.

4. **Implementing New Strategies**: Gain insights into practical techniques such as mindfulness, habit stacking, and the use of visual aids like tables and charts to track progress and stay motivated.

5. **Consistency and Perseverance**: Understand the significance of consistency in breaking negative habits and how to maintain motivation and resilience in the face of setbacks. Unbroken focus is the key to your success in breaking negative habits.

By the end of this chapter, you will be equipped with the knowledge and tools needed to dismantle negative habits and build positive ones in their place. Through self-awareness, strategic planning, and unwavering commitment, you can break free from the chains of detrimental behaviours and pave the way for a healthier, more productive life.

Step 1: Identify the Habit and Its Triggers

Habit	Trigger	Replacement Behaviour
Procrastination	Feeling overwhelmed	Break tasks into smaller steps
Nail biting	Stress or boredom	Use a stress ball
Excessive snacking	Watching TV	Drink water or tea
Negative self-talk	Facing failure	Practice positive affirmations

Step 2: Develop a Plan and Set Goals

Table: SMART Goals for Breaking Negative Habits

Habit	Specific Goal	Measurable	Achievable	Relevant	Time-bound
Procrastination	Complete daily to-do list	Track completed tasks	Yes	Improve productivity	Within 30 days
Nail biting	Reduce nail biting incidents to zero	Count incidents daily	Yes	Improve nail health	Within 21 days
Excessive snacking	Replace snacks with healthy alternatives	Track snack choices	Yes	Improve diet	Within 4 weeks
Negative self-talk	Write 5 positive affirmations daily	Affirmation journal	Yes	Improve self-esteem	Within 2 weeks

Step 3: Monitor Progress and Adjust Strategies

Table: Weekly Progress Tracker

Week	Habit	Replacement Behaviour Used	Success Rate (%)	Comments
1	Procrastination	Task breakdown	70%	Need to prioritise tasks better
1	Nail biting	Stress ball	60%	Use stress ball more frequently
1	Excessive snacking	Drinking water	50%	Increase water intake
1	Negative self-talk	Positive affirmations	80%	Affirmations are helpful
2	Procrastination	Task breakdown	80%	Improvement noted
2	Nail biting	Stress ball	70%	Slight decrease in incidents
2	Excessive snacking	Drinking water	60%	Healthy snack choices
2	Negative self-talk	Positive affirmations	85%	Continues to be effective

Step 4: Reflect and Reward

Table: Reflection and Rewards

Week	Habit	Reflections	Rewards
1	Procrastination	Need to better manage time	Watch a movie
1	Nail biting	Stress ball usage needs to increase	Buy a new nail polish
1	Excessive snacking	Need to be more conscious of choices	Treat with a healthy dessert
1	Negative self-talk	Affirmations are effective	Enjoy a relaxing bath
2	Procrastination	Improvement noted	Go out for a fun activity
2	Nail biting	Incidents decreased slightly	Buy a small gift for self
2	Excessive snacking	Making healthier snack choices	Try a new healthy recipe
2	Negative self-talk	Positive affirmations help	Enjoy a favourite hobby

Implementation Steps
(*These steps may be repeated for several practices*)

Breaking negative habits can be challenging, but with the right strategies and mindset, it is achievable. Here are some effective strategies to help you break negative habits, along with practical examples to illustrate each point:

Identify Triggers

Pay attention to the triggers or cues that prompt your negative habits. These triggers could be specific situations, emotions, people, or environments. By identifying your triggers, you can become more aware of when and why you engage in the negative habit, making it easier to interrupt the pattern.

Example: If you find yourself smoking whenever you feel stressed at work, recognise stress as a trigger. Keep a log of instances when you smoke and note the circumstances that led to it.

Replace with Positive Alternatives

Instead of simply trying to stop a negative habit, replace it with a positive alternative. This substitution provides a healthier outlet for your needs.

Example: If you tend to stress-eat junk food, replace it with healthier snacks like fruits or nuts. Additionally, engage in stress-relief activities such as meditation, exercise, or deep breathing exercises whenever you feel the urge to snack.

Set Clear Goals

Clearly define your goals for breaking the negative habit and outline the steps you will take to achieve them. Make your goals specific, measurable, achievable, relevant, and time-bound (SMART).

Example: Instead of setting a vague goal like "stop procrastinating," specify "Complete my daily work tasks by 5 PM every day for the next month." Outline steps such as breaking tasks into smaller pieces, setting timers for focused work periods, and rewarding yourself for meeting your goals.

Use Habit Reversal Training
Habit reversal training is a cognitive-behavioural technique that involves identifying the cues and rewards associated with a habit and then consciously replacing the routine with a more positive behaviour.

Example: If nail-biting is your habit, identify when and why you do it (e.g., when anxious). Replace the nail-biting routine with squeezing a stress ball or using a fidget spinner to keep your hands occupied.

Practice Mindfulness
Mindfulness involves paying attention to the present moment without judgment. By practicing mindfulness, you can become more aware of your thoughts, feelings, and behaviours, making it easier to recognise and interrupt negative habits as they arise.

Example: Practice mindful eating by paying close attention to the taste, texture, and sensation of your food. This can help reduce mindless snacking.

Utilise Social Support
Share your goals with friends, family members, or a support group who can provide encouragement, accountability, and guidance. Surrounding yourself with supportive individuals who understand your challenges can make the process of breaking negative habits feel less daunting and more manageable.

Example: Join a fitness group or a smoking cessation program. Having a workout buddy or a quit-smoking partner can provide mutual support and accountability.

Take One Step at a Time
Breaking a negative habit is often a gradual process, and setbacks are a natural part of the journey. Be patient with yourself and celebrate small victories along the way. Focus on progress rather than perfection and recognise that change takes time.

Example: If you're trying to reduce screen time, start by cutting down 15 minutes each day rather than eliminating it all at once. Celebrate each week you successfully reduce your screen time.

Address Underlying Issues
Negative habits often stem from underlying emotional, psychological, or environmental factors. Take the time to explore and address these underlying issues, whether it's stress, boredom, low self-esteem, or past trauma. Seeking

support from a therapist or counsellor can be valuable in uncovering root causes.

Example: If you drink alcohol to cope with anxiety, consider seeking therapy to address the anxiety itself. Cognitive-behavioural therapy can be particularly effective in dealing with underlying issues.

Practice Self-Compassion
Be kind and compassionate with yourself throughout the process of breaking negative habits. Recognise that change is hard, and setbacks are normal. Treat yourself with the same kindness and understanding that you would offer to a friend facing the same.

Example: If you slip up and fall back into a negative habit, instead of berating yourself, acknowledge that mistakes are part of the process. Reflect on what led to the slip-up and use it as a learning experience to strengthen your resolve.

By implementing these strategies consistently and with determination, you can break free from negative habits and cultivate healthier, more positive behaviours that align with your values and goals. Remember that change is not change until you change, and there is no better person to start the change process and road to recovery than you.

27

How to Create New Positive Habits

Creating New Positive Habits

A Pathway to Lasting Change
Establishing new positive habits is a cornerstone of personal development and a key to unlocking a more fulfilling, productive, and healthy life. While the process of habit formation can be challenging, it is also immensely rewarding, offering a pathway to lasting change and improvement. By understanding the mechanics of habit formation, setting clear and achievable goals, and implementing consistent strategies, you can cultivate behaviours that support your aspirations and enhance your well-being.

In this chapter, we will guide you through the essential steps to create and sustain positive habits. We will explore the science behind habit formation, provide practical advice for identifying and reinforcing new behaviours, and offer illustrated guides and tables to help you visualise and track your progress. This structured approach will empower you to turn your goals into actionable steps, ensuring that your new habits become an integral part of your daily routine and everyday life.

Our exploration will include

Understanding Habit Formation: Gain insights into the habit loop, cue, routine, and reward—and how it applies to developing positive habits.

Identifying Triggers and Cues: Learn to recognise the triggers that can prompt positive behaviour changes and how to design your environment to support your new habits.

Setting Clear Goals: The importance of setting specific, measurable, attainable, relevant, and time-bound (SMART) goals that align with your values.

Consistent Strategies for Success: Explore effective techniques such as habit stacking, implementation intentions, and the use of visual aids like habit trackers to reinforce new habits.

Overcoming Obstacles and Staying Motivated: Understand common challenges in habit formation and strategies to overcome them, ensuring that you stay motivated and committed to your goals.

Reviewing and Reflecting on Progress: Learn the importance of regular reflection and adjustment to ensure your new habits are sustainable and continue to support your long-term objectives.

By the end of this chapter, you will have a comprehensive toolkit for creating and maintaining positive habits. Through strategic planning, consistent practice, and mindful reflection, you can transform your daily routines and achieve meaningful, lasting change in your life.

Step 1: Identify Desired Habits and Triggers

Positive Habit	Trigger	Current Routine	New Routine
Daily Exercise	Morning wake-up	Stay in bed for a while	10-minute morning workout
Reading Daily	After dinner	Watch TV	Read a book for 30 minutes
Healthy Eating	Lunchtime	Fast food	Prepare a healthy meal
Meditation	Before bed	Scroll through phone	10-minute meditation session

Step 2: Set SMART Goals

Table: SMART Goals for Creating Positive Habits

Habit	Specific Goal	Measurable	Achievable	Relevant	Time-bound
Daily Exercise	Exercise for 30 minutes every morning	Track daily exercise duration	Yes	Improve fitness	Within 4 weeks
Reading Daily	Read 20 pages of a book each evening	Count pages read	Yes	Increase knowledge	Within 30 days
Healthy Eating	Prepare healthy meals for lunch daily	Track meals prepared	Yes	Improve diet	Within 3 weeks
Meditation	Meditate for 10 minutes before bed	Track meditation sessions	Yes	Reduce stress	Within 2 weeks

Step 3: Implement and Monitor Progress

Table: Weekly Progress Tracker

Week	Habit	New Routine Implemented	Success Rate (%)	Comments
1	Daily Exercise	10-minute morning workout	80%	Need to increase duration
1	Reading Daily	Read a book for 30 minutes	70%	Need to be more consistent
1	Healthy Eating	Prepare a healthy meal	60%	Prep meals in advance
1	Meditation	10-minute meditation	90%	Very relaxing
2	Daily Exercise	20-minute morning workout	85%	Feeling more energetic
2	Reading Daily	Read a book for 30 minutes	75%	Better focus
2	Healthy Eating	Prepare a healthy meal	70%	Experiment with new recipes
2	Meditation	10-minute meditation	95%	Helps with sleep

Step 4: Reflect and Adjust

Table: Reflection and Adjustments

Week	Habit	Reflections	Adjustments
1	Daily Exercise	Need to gradually increase duration	Add 5 minutes each week
1	Reading Daily	Sometimes skip reading	Set a specific reading time
1	Healthy Eating	Difficult to find time for meal prep	Prep meals on weekends
1	Meditation	Very beneficial for stress relief	Continue as is
2	Daily Exercise	More energy and better mood	Increase to 30 minutes
2	Reading Daily	Enjoying the new routine	Continue with set reading time
2	Healthy Eating	Enjoying new recipes	Try new healthy recipes weekly
2	Meditation	Improved sleep quality	Continue as is

Implementation Steps (Standard)

Creating new, positive habits is a powerful way to improve your life and achieve your goals. Whether you want to enhance your physical health, boost your productivity, or cultivate a more positive mindset, establishing new habits can serve as the foundation for lasting change:

Start Small
When embarking on the journey of habit formation, beginning with small, manageable changes is crucial. This approach allows you to build confidence and gradually increase your commitment.

Example: If you want to start exercising regularly, don't overwhelm yourself with the goal of hitting the gym for an hour every day. Instead, start by committing to a 10-minute walk after dinner three times a week. Once this becomes a routine, you can gradually increase the duration or frequency.

Set Specific Goals
Define your goals clearly to provide direction and clarity. Make sure your goals are Specific, Measurable, Achievable, Relevant, and Time-bound.

Example: Instead of saying "I want to read more," specify your goal: "I will read one book per month."

Establish a Routine
Incorporating new habits into your daily routine makes it easier to remember and implement them. Choose a specific time, or location to trigger you.

Example: If you want to meditate daily, set aside a time every morning immediately after you wake up. Designate a quiet spot in your home for meditation. By linking meditation to waking up, you create a clear routine that becomes automatic over time.

Use Habit Stacking

Habit stacking involves pairing a new habit with an existing one, making it easier to remember and implement. This technique leverages the power of established habits to help you build new ones.

Example: If you already have a habit of making coffee every morning, you could stack a new habit of stretching for five minutes right after you brew your coffee. This connection between two habits makes it easier to remember to do the new activity.

Stay Consistent

Consistency is vital for habit formation. Committing to practice the new habit daily, even if it's for a short period, helps reinforce the behaviour.

Example: If you're trying to drink more water, set a goal to drink one glass of water each morning upon waking. You can track this habit using a habit-tracking app or a simple checklist on your fridge.

Learn to Reward Yourself

Incentivising your progress is a powerful way to reinforce positive behaviour. Choose rewards that resonate with you and are aligned with your goals.

Example: If you complete your daily writing goal for a week, treat yourself to a movie night or a favourite dessert. This creates a positive association with the new habit and motivates you to continue.

Anticipate Setbacks
Recognise that setbacks are a natural part of the habit-forming process. Anticipating challenges can prepare you to respond constructively when obstacles arise.

Example: If you know that evenings tend to be busy, plan for this by scheduling your workout in the morning. If you miss a day, don't dwell on it. Instead, develop a strategy to get back on track, like having a quick 5-minute home workout before a busy day.

Stay Flexible
Be open to adapting and adjusting your approach as necessary. What works for one person may not work for another, and it's important to find the strategies that resonate with you.

Example: If you initially set a goal to read for 30 minutes every night before bed but find you're too tired, try changing it to reading for 10 minutes in the morning instead. Flexibility allows you to create a habit that fits your lifestyle better.

Practical Steps for Creating New, Positive Habits

1. Daily Reflection:
Spend a few minutes each day reflecting on your new habit. This practice helps reinforce your commitment and allows you to identify any challenges.

Example: At the end of the day, journal about your progress. Write down what went well, what challenges you faced, and how you felt about your efforts. This self-reflection enhances your awareness.

2. Create Visual Reminders:
Use visual cues to remind yourself of your new habits. This can be a sticky note, or an app notification.

Example: Place a sticky note on your bathroom mirror that says, "Drink water!" or set an alarm on your phone labelled "Time to meditate!" Visual reminders can prompt you to stay committed.

3. Join a Group or Community:
Engaging with others who share similar goals can provide support and accountability.

Example: If your goal is to exercise more, join a local walking group or an online fitness community. Sharing your experiences with others can motivate you and provide new insights.

4. Practice Gratitude:
Incorporating gratitude into your routine can enhance your motivation and overall mindset.

Example: At the end of each week, write down three things you're grateful for related to your new habit. For instance, if you've started journaling, reflect on how it has improved your mood or clarity of thought.

5. Be Patient:
Remember that creating lasting change takes time. Be patient with yourself as you adjust to your new habits.

Example: If you slip up, acknowledge it and move forward without guilt. Recognise that building habits is a journey, and progress may be gradual.

Creating new positive habits is a transformative journey that requires patience, dedication, and resilience. As you embark on this path, it's crucial to remember that meaningful change is a gradual process. The effort you invest in understanding habit formation, setting clear goals, and consistently applying effective strategies will pay off over time, leading to lasting improvements in your life. The road to establishing positive habits is not always smooth, but each step forward, no matter how small, brings you closer to your goals. Celebrate your progress, acknowledge your efforts, and be kind to yourself when setbacks occur. These moments are opportunities for learning and growth, reinforcing your commitment to creating a better you.

As you cultivate new habits, you will notice profound changes in your daily life. These habits will not only enhance your productivity and well-being but also align closely with your values and aspirations, leading to a more fulfilling and enriched existence. Each positive habit you establish acts as a building block, contributing to a foundation of personal growth and resilience. The journey of creating new positive habits is an ongoing process of self-discovery and improvement. Stay persistent, remain determined, and trust in the process. With time and effort, you will find that your new habits become a natural and integral part of your life.

28

Breaking free from Addiction

Breaking free from Addiction

Overcoming addiction is a complex and challenging journey that requires a comprehensive and multi-faceted approach. Success in breaking free from addictions hinges on understanding the underlying triggers, setting realistic and achievable goals, developing effective coping strategies, and seeking the necessary support from professionals and loved ones. This process involves both physical and psychological transformation, demanding perseverance and resilience. Addictions, whether they be to substances, behaviours, or activities, can deeply impact every aspect of an individual's life. They often stem from a combination of genetic, environmental, and psychological factors, making each person's experience with addiction unique.

Recognising this complexity is the first step in creating a tailored plan that addresses your specific needs and circumstances. In this chapter, we provide an illustrated guide designed to help you navigate the path to recovery. This guide includes detailed tables and practical tools to help you identify your triggers, set meaningful goals, develop robust coping mechanisms, and build a strong support network. Each strategy is presented with clear, actionable steps, empowering you to take control of your journey.

When you integrate these strategies into your daily life, you will gradually break the cycle of addiction and pave the way for a healthier, more fulfilling future. Remember, overcoming addiction is not just about quitting a substance or behaviour; it's about creating a sustainable and positive lifestyle change. This chapter aims to equip you with the knowledge and resources needed to achieve lasting recovery and reclaim your life. As already pointed out, some of these strategies will cross over various chapters as they are necessary for success in each case. Repetitive action of a good practice that yields multiple results is always positive.

Step 1: Identify Triggers and Patterns

Addiction Type	Trigger	Current Response	New Response
Smoking	Stressful situations	Smoke a cigarette	Deep breathing exercises
Alcohol	Social gatherings	Drink alcohol	Drink non-alcoholic beverages
Overeating	Feeling bored or lonely	Eat junk food	Engage in a hobby
Internet Use	Avoiding work or chores	Browse social media	Take a short walk

Step 2: Set SMART Goals

Table: SMART Goals for Breaking Addictions

Addiction Type	Specific Goal	Measurable	Achievable	Relevant	Time-bound
Smoking	Reduce to 5 cigarettes per day in the first month	Count daily cigarettes	Yes	Improve health	Within 1 month
Alcohol	Limit to 2 drinks per week	Track weekly drinks	Yes	Better relationships	Within 2 months
Overeating	Replace one junk food meal with a healthy meal	Track meals	Yes	Weight loss	Within 3 weeks
Internet Use	Limit social media to 1 hour per day	Monitor daily usage	Yes	Increase productivity	Within 2 weeks

Step 3: Develop Coping Strategies

Table: Coping Strategies for Addiction Triggers

Trigger	Coping Strategy	Implementation Plan
Stressful situations	Deep breathing, meditation	Practice daily, especially when stressed
Social gatherings	Drink non-alcoholic beverages, find sober friends	Bring own drinks, join sober groups
Feeling bored/lonely	Engage in hobbies, exercise	Schedule hobby time, join activity groups
Avoiding work/chores	Set timers for breaks, take short walks	Use timer apps, plan short walks

Step 4: Seek Support and Accountability

Table: Support Systems

Support Type	Description	Action Plan
Family Support	Share goals with family, ask for encouragement	Regular check-ins with family members
Professional Help	Seek therapy or counselling	Schedule weekly therapy sessions
Support Groups	Join addiction support groups	Attend weekly meetings
Accountability Partner	Find a friend to share progress and setbacks	Regular check-ins with accountability partner

Step 5: Monitor Progress and Adjust

Table: Weekly Progress Tracker

Week	Addiction Type	Goal Achieved	Success Rate (%)	Comments
1	Smoking	Yes	80%	Need more strategies for stress
1	Alcohol	No	50%	Find more non-alcoholic options
1	Overeating	Yes	70%	Continue finding healthy recipes
1	Internet Use	Yes	90%	Very effective using timer apps
2	Smoking	Yes	85%	Deep breathing is helpful
2	Alcohol	Yes	60%	Better at social gatherings
2	Overeating	Yes	80%	Enjoying new healthy meals
2	Internet Use	Yes	95%	Increased productivity

Understanding the Nature of Addiction

Understanding the nature of addiction is crucial for effectively addressing and overcoming this complex and pervasive issue. Addiction is a chronic, relapsing disorder characterised by compulsive drug seeking and use, despite harmful consequences. It profoundly affects the brain's structure and function, leading to changes in behaviour, cognition, and emotional regulation. This chapter explores key aspects of addiction and provides practical examples to illustrate.

Brain Chemistry
Addiction fundamentally alters the brain's neurochemistry, particularly in areas involved in reward, motivation, learning, and decision-making. Drugs of abuse hijack the brain's natural reward system, flooding it with dopamine and creating an artificial sense of pleasure and euphoria. Over time, repeated drug use desensitises the brain's reward circuitry, leading to tolerance and the need for increasing amounts of the substance to achieve the same effect.

Example: Imagine the brain as a well-tuned orchestra where dopamine is a key player. Initially, a small amount of drug use creates an overwhelming flood of dopamine, akin to adding a powerful new instrument to the orchestra. Over time, the brain adjusts by dampening its natural response, requiring more of the drug to achieve the same effect, similar to needing more musicians to produce the same volume of sound.

Neuroplasticity
Chronic drug use induces neuroplastic changes in the brain, rewiring neural circuits and reinforcing addictive behaviours. These changes contribute to the compulsive nature of addiction, making it difficult for someone to control their drug use despite negative consequences. The brain's plasticity also

means it can adapt and reorganise in response to environmental influences, including treatment interventions and behavioural changes.

Example: Think of the brain as a densely wooded forest. Regular drug use creates well-worn paths through this forest, making it easy to follow these routes. Recovery involves forging new paths, which can be challenging initially but become easier as these new routes are repeatedly travelled.

Psychological Factors
Addiction often co-occurs with underlying psychological issues such as trauma, stress, anxiety, depression, or low self-esteem. These factors can contribute to the development and maintenance of addictive behaviours, serving as coping mechanisms or ways of self-medicating emotional pain or distress. Addressing these underlying psychological issues is essential for comprehensive addiction treatment and long-term recovery.

Example: Consider addiction as a fire that can be fuelled by psychological distress. Stress, trauma, and anxiety are the kindling that can ignite and sustain the flames of addiction. Comprehensive treatment must address both the fire and the kindling to be effective.

Genetics and Environment
Both genetic and environmental factors play significant roles in the development of addiction. Genetic predisposition

accounts for about half of an individual's susceptibility to addiction, while environmental factors such as exposure to stress, trauma, peer pressure, socioeconomic status, and availability of drugs also influence addiction risk. Understanding the interplay between genetic vulnerabilities and environmental triggers is essential for personalised treatment approaches.

Example: Think of genetics as the soil in which a plant (person) grows. Rich, fertile soil might predispose a plant to grow vigorously (high susceptibility to addiction), while poor, rocky soil might do the opposite. Environmental factors like water, sunlight, and pests further influence the plant's growth, in the same way that external factors affect an individual's risk for addiction.

Chronic Disease Model

Addiction is increasingly recognised as a chronic disease of the brain, akin to medical conditions such as diabetes or hypertension. Like these diseases, addiction is characterised by cycles of relapse and remission, requiring ongoing management and support. Viewing addiction through the lens of a chronic disease model helps reduce stigma, promote empathy, and emphasise the importance of long-term treatment and recovery efforts.

Example: Just as a person with diabetes must manage their condition with lifestyle changes, medication, and regular check-ups, someone with addiction requires ongoing strategies, support, and treatment to maintain recovery.

Behavioural Reinforcement
Addiction involves powerful behavioural reinforcement mechanisms, where cues associated with drug use trigger intense cravings and compulsive drug-seeking behaviours. These cues can be external (e.g., drug paraphernalia, social settings) or internal (e.g., stress, emotions), and they contribute to the cycle of addiction by reinforcing maladaptive behaviours and undermining efforts to quit.

Example: Picture Pavlov's dogs, who salivated at the sound of a bell because they associated it with food. Similarly, an addict might crave drugs at the sight of a certain place or person because of past associations with drug use.

Social and Cultural Factors
Social and cultural factors also influence addiction patterns, including attitudes toward substance use, peer influences, societal norms, and access to treatment and support services. Cultural beliefs and practices may shape individuals' perceptions of addiction, impact help-seeking behaviours, and influence treatment outcomes. Understanding these factors is essential for developing culturally competent and inclusive addiction interventions.

Example: In some cultures, drinking alcohol is a common social activity, making it more challenging for someone to recognise problematic drinking behaviours and seek help. Conversely, cultures with strong anti-drug norms may encourage individuals to hide their addiction, complicating their access to treatment and prolonging their wellbeing.

Practical Strategies for Addressing Addiction

Make the Decision to Change
The journey to recovery starts with a personal decision to change. Acknowledging the problem and committing to change is the first critical step.

Example: Sarah, a recovering alcoholic, made the decision to change after realising her drinking was affecting her work and relationships. She sought help from a therapist and joined a support group, committing to her recovery process.

Seek Professional Help
Professional treatment can provide the structure and support needed to address addiction comprehensively. This may include therapy, medical treatment, and support groups.

Example: John struggled with opioid addiction and decided to enter a rehabilitation program. At the Rehabilitation Centre, he received medical detox, counselling, and learned coping strategies to manage his cravings and avoid relapse.

Build a Support Network
Having a strong support network can provide emotional support, accountability, and encouragement during the recovery process.

Example: Emily found strength in her recovery by joining a local Narcotics Anonymous group. The support from others who understood her struggles helped her stay committed to her sobriety.

Develop Healthy Coping Mechanisms
Learning new ways to cope with stress and emotional pain is crucial for preventing relapse.

Example: Mark, who had a gambling addiction, started practicing yoga and meditation to manage his stress and anxiety. These healthy outlets helped him resist the urge to gamble.

Set Realistic Goals
Setting achievable and realistic goals can help individuals track their progress and stay motivated.

Example: Lisa, who wanted to quit smoking, set a goal to reduce her cigarette intake gradually. She used nicotine patches and counselling to support her journey, celebrating each milestone along the way.

Address Underlying Issues
Addressing the psychological factors underlying addiction is essential for long-term recovery.

Example: Muntu, who struggled with alcohol addiction, realised his drinking was a way to cope with unresolved trauma. Through therapy, he worked through his past experiences and developed healthier coping strategies.

Practice Self-Compassion
Recovery is a challenging process, and practicing self-compassion can help individuals stay resilient and motivated.

Example: After a relapse, Maria felt discouraged but reminded herself that setbacks are part of the journey. She forgave herself, sought support, and continued her path to recovery with renewed determination.

A comprehensive understanding of the multifaceted nature of addiction, including its biological, psychological, social, and cultural dimensions, can help us develop more effective prevention, intervention, and treatment strategies that address the complex needs of individuals struggling with addiction. This holistic approach recognises addiction as a complex and nuanced phenomenon that requires compassionate, evidence-based interventions tailored to the unique circumstances and experiences of everyone. Understanding the nature of addiction is the first step towards effective intervention and recovery. By acknowledging the complexity of addiction and implementing strategies that address its various dimensions, you and your support networks can work towards lasting change and a healthier, more fulfilling life. Remember, change is possible, and every step towards breaking free from addiction brings you closer to the life you want. With persistence and determination, you can achieve the success you seek, and your last word shall be victory.

29

Breaking free from Phobias

Breaking Free from Phobias

Phobias are intense, irrational fears of specific objects, activities, or situations that can significantly impact one's life. These fears can be debilitating, preventing individuals from engaging in everyday activities and experiencing life to the fullest. In this chapter, we will explore strategies to break free from phobias, using practical examples and illustrations to guide you on your journey to overcoming these fears.

Understanding Phobias
Phobias are classified into three main types:

Specific Phobias: Fear of specific objects or situations (e.g., spiders, heights).

Social Phobia (Social Anxiety Disorder): Fear of social situations and being judged or embarrassed.

Agoraphobia: Fear of situations where escape might be difficult or help unavailable (e.g., crowded places, open spaces).

Understanding and accepting the type of phobia you have is the first step toward overcoming it.

Identifying Triggers

Identifying the triggers of your phobia is crucial. Keep a journal to track situations, objects, or thoughts that induce fear. For example:

Specific Phobia Example: If you fear spiders, note down when and where you encounter them and how you feel.

Social Phobia Example: If you fear public speaking, note down instances when you felt anxious about speaking in front of a group.

Illustration: Create a table to log your triggers.

Date	Trigger	Location	Physical Symptoms	Emotional Response
27-07-2024	Seeing a spider	Bathroom	Sweating, trembling	Panic, dread
09-08-2024	Public speaking	Office meeting	Racing heart	Anxiety, fear

Gradual Exposure Therapy

Gradual exposure therapy involves slowly and systematically exposing yourself to the feared object or situation. This technique helps desensitise you to the fear over time.

Steps for Exposure Therapy:

List Hierarchy of Fears: Rank your fears from least to most terrifying.

Example: Fear of spiders
- Seeing a picture of a spider
- Watching a video of a spider
- Being in the same room as a spider
- Holding a toy spider
- Being near a live spider

Start Small: Begin with the least frightening scenario. Spend time with this exposure until your anxiety decreases.

Example: Look at pictures of spiders for a few minutes each day until you feel comfortable.

Progress Gradually: Move up your hierarchy, tackling each level of fear.

Example: Watch videos of spiders, then progress to being in the same room as a spider.

Illustration: Create a visual hierarchy ladder.

Holding a toy spider
↑
Being in the same room as a spider
↑
Watching a video of a spider
↑
Seeing a picture of a spider

Cognitive-Behavioural Techniques
Cognitive-behavioural therapy (CBT) helps challenge and change negative thought patterns associated with phobias.

Steps for CBT:
Identify Negative Thoughts: Recognise thoughts that cause fear.

Example: "Spiders are dangerous and will bite me."
Challenge These Thoughts: Question the validity of these thoughts.

Example: "Most spiders are harmless and do their best to avoid humans."

Replace with Positive Thoughts: Substitute negative thoughts with rational, calming ones.

Example: "I can handle seeing a spider. It's not as dangerous as I think."

Illustration: Create a thought log

Situation	Negative Thought	Rational Thought
Seeing a spider	"It will bite me and harm me."	"Most spiders are harmless."
Public speaking	"Everyone will judge me."	"People are interested in my ideas."

Relaxation Techniques
Incorporating relaxation techniques can help manage the physical symptoms of phobias.

Deep Breathing: Practice slow, deep breaths to calm your nervous system.

Example: Inhale for 4 Sec, hold for 4, exhale for 4.

Progressive Muscle Relaxation: Tense and relax different muscle groups to release tension.

Example: Start with your toes and work your way up to your head.

Mindfulness Meditation: Focus on the present moment to reduce anxiety.

Example: Sit quietly and pay attention to your breathing, letting go of fearful thoughts.

Illustration: Include diagrams of deep breathing and progressive muscle relaxation techniques.

Deep Breathing
1. Inhale deeply through your nose (4 seconds)
2. Hold your breath (4 seconds)
3. Exhale slowly through your mouth (4 seconds)

Seeking Professional Help
Sometimes, overcoming phobias requires professional assistance. Therapists and counsellors trained in CBT and exposure therapy can provide personalised strategies and support.

Finding a therapist: Look for licensed professionals specialising in anxiety disorders.

Support Groups: Join groups where you can share experiences and strategies with others facing similar fears in a safe environment.

Illustration: Include a checklist for seeking professional help. Here is a short-list to help:

Steps to Find Professional Help
1. Research licensed therapists specialising in phobias.
2. Check their credentials and reviews.
3. Schedule an initial consultation.
4. Discuss your phobia and therapy plan.
5. Commit to regular sessions and follow through.

Breaking free from phobias is a challenging but achievable goal. Understanding your triggers, gradually exposing yourself to fears, employing cognitive-behavioural techniques, practicing relaxation methods, and seeking professional help if needed, will help you overcome these debilitating fears. Remember, progress takes time and patience, but with dedication, you can reclaim your life.

Illustration: Let us conclude this chapter with a motivational quote and a reminder of the benefits of overcoming phobias - "Fear is only as deep as the mind allows." - Japanese Proverb

Benefits of Overcoming Phobias
- Increased confidence and self-esteem.
- Enhanced ability to participate in daily activities.
- Improved relationships and social interactions.
- Greater overall quality of life.

30

Cognitive Behavioural Therapy (CBT)

Cognitive Behavioural Therapy (CBT)

Cognitive Behavioural Therapy a highly effective therapeutic approach that focuses on identifying and changing negative thought patterns and behaviours. It is widely used to treat various mental health conditions, including anxiety, depression, and stress-related disorders. The core principle of CBT is that our thoughts, feelings, and behaviours are interconnected, and by altering one, we can influence the others. This chapter provides practical applications of CBT techniques, illustrated with examples to help you integrate these strategies into your daily life and routines. CBT is a widely used therapeutic approach that focuses on identifying and challenging negative thought patterns and behaviours. Recognising and modifying maladaptive cognitive processes, can help you rewire neural pathways associated with harmful behaviours and beliefs, replacing them with more adaptive and constructive ones. CBT is based on the idea that our thoughts (cognitions) affect our emotions and behaviours. By identifying and challenging irrational or maladaptive thoughts, we can develop healthier thinking patterns and behaviours. Here are some key CBT elements:

Mindfulness Meditation
Mindfulness meditation involves cultivating present-moment awareness and non-judgmental acceptance of thoughts, emotions, and sensations. Regular mindfulness practice can strengthen neural pathways associated with attention,

emotional regulation, and self-awareness, promoting resilience and reducing reactivity to stressors and triggers.

Neurofeedback
Neurofeedback is a form of biofeedback that uses real-time monitoring of brain activity to teach self-regulation of neural function. By providing individuals with feedback about their brainwave patterns, neurofeedback can help them learn to modulate their brain activity and promote healthier neural functioning, leading to improvements in attention, mood, and behaviour.

Physical Exercise
Regular physical exercise has been shown to enhance neuroplasticity and promote the growth of new neurons and synaptic connections in the brain. Aerobic exercise has been linked to improvements in cognitive function, mood regulation, and stress resilience, likely due to its effects on neurotrophic factors and neurotransmitter systems.

Learning and Intellectual Stimulation
Engaging in intellectually stimulating activities such as reading, learning new skills, or participating in challenging mental tasks can promote neuroplasticity and enhance cognitive function. By exposing the brain to novel experiences and information, individuals can strengthen existing neural connections and form new ones, facilitating learning and memory consolidation.

Social Connection and Support

Social interaction and meaningful relationships play a crucial role in brain health and neuroplasticity. Positive social experiences, such as empathy, trust, and emotional support, can stimulate the release of oxytocin and other neurotransmitters associated with bonding and reward, promoting neural growth and resilience. Conversely, social isolation and loneliness have been linked to adverse effects on brain structure and function.

Cognitive Training Programs

Various cognitive training programs and brain exercises are designed to target specific cognitive functions, such as attention, memory, and executive function. These programs often utilise computer-based tasks and games to challenge and stimulate neural networks, promoting adaptive changes in brain structure and function.

Psychoeducation and Psychotherapy

Learning about the brain's plasticity and the mechanisms underlying behaviour can empower individuals to take an active role in rewiring their neural pathways. Psychoeducation, combined with psychotherapeutic interventions such as psychoanalysis, motivational interviewing, or acceptance and commitment therapy (ACT), can help individuals develop insight into their thought patterns and behaviour and facilitate lasting changes in neural connectivity. Incorporating these strategies into daily life and treatment approaches, will help you harness the power of neuroplasticity to rewire maladaptive neural pathways, promote positive changes in behaviour and cognition, and enhance overall well-being and resilience. While rewiring neural pathways requires time, effort, and persistence, the brain's capacity for change offers hope and potential for growth, recovery, and transformation.

Learn from Mistakes and Seek Support
Embrace failures and setbacks as opportunities for growth and learning. Instead of dwelling on past mistakes, reflect on what you can learn from them and how you can use that knowledge to inform future actions. Approach challenges with a growth mindset, viewing them as stepping stones on the path to personal development. Reach out to supportive friends, family members, or mental health professionals for guidance and encouragement. Sharing your struggles with trusted others can provide validation, perspective, and a sense of belonging, reinforcing feelings of self-compassion and worthiness. Cultivating self-compassion is an ongoing journey that requires patience, practice, and commitment. By incorporating these strategies into your daily life and treating yourself with kindness and understanding, you can foster a deeper sense of self-compassion and acceptance, leading to greater resilience, well-being, and fulfilment.

Set Boundaries and Prioritise Self-Care
Honor your own needs and boundaries by prioritising self-care and self-compassion. Make time for activities that nourish your body, mind, and spirit, whether it's spending time

in nature, engaging in creative pursuits, or seeking support from others. Remember that you are not alone in experiencing suffering or challenges. Acknowledge that all human beings face struggles and setbacks at various points in their lives. Recognising our shared humanity can help foster feelings of connection and empathy, reducing feelings of isolation or self-blame. Understand that you cannot set boundaries on other people as those would be unenforceable boundaries. The only boundaries you can influence and have the power to enforce, are the ones you set on yourself.

Practical Applications of CBT

Identifying Negative Thoughts: Recognising automatic negative thoughts that contribute to emotional distress.

Example: Sarah feels anxious about an upcoming presentation at work. Her automatic thought is, "I'm going to mess up, and everyone will think I'm incompetent." Fear of failure has made her anxious.

Illustration: A thought record worksheet where Sarah writes down the situation, her automatic thought, the emotions she feels, and an alternative thought. This way, she can easily identify her negative thought patterns and address them.

Situation	Automatic Thought	Emotion	Alternative Thought
Work presentation	"I'm going to mess up."	Anxiety (8/10)	"I have prepared well and can handle this."
	"Everyone will think I'm incompetent."	Fear (7/10)	"Everyone makes mistakes, and I can recover."

Challenging Negative Thoughts: Evaluating the validity of these thoughts and considering alternative perspectives.

Technique: Cognitive Restructuring

Identify Cognitive Distortions: Sarah recognises that she is engaging in "catastrophising" and "mind reading."
Evidence for and Against: She lists evidence supporting and contradicting her negative thought.
Balanced Thought: Sarah formulates a more balanced perspective.
Evidence for: "I did stumble during my last presentation."
Evidence against: "I received positive feedback overall, and I have practiced extensively for this one."
Balanced Thought: "While I might make a mistake, I am well-prepared, and I have succeeded in the past."
Behavioural Activation:
Engaging in activities that align with positive outcomes and personal goals.

Example: John feels depressed and has lost interest in activities he used to enjoy.
Technique: Activity Scheduling
List Enjoyable Activities: John lists activities he used to find enjoyable (e.g., jogging, reading, meeting friends).
Schedule Activities: He schedules these activities throughout the week.

Illustration: John's weekly activity schedule.

Day	Morning	Afternoon	Evening
Monday	Jogging	Work	Read a book
Tuesday	Work	Lunch with friend	Work
Wednesday	Work	Jogging	Call a friend
Thursday	Work	Reading	Watch a movie
Friday	Work	Work	Dinner with family
Saturday	Jogging	Shopping	Meet friends
Sunday	Relax	Family outing	Prepare for week

Problem-Solving:
Develop effective strategies for specific challenges.
Example: Emily is overwhelmed by a complex project at work.
Technique: Problem-Solving Steps
Define the Problem: Break down the project into smaller, manageable tasks.

Generate Solutions: Brainstorm possible solutions for each task.

Evaluate Solutions: Assess the feasibility and potential outcomes of each solution.

Implement the Best Solution: Choose the best solution and implement it.

Review and Adjust: Evaluate the effectiveness of the solution and adjust as needed.

Illustration: Emily's problem-solving chart.

Task	Possible Solutions	Evaluation	Chosen Solution	Outcome
Research	Online research, library, consult experts	Feasible and thorough	Consult experts	Comprehensive information
Drafting	Outline first, write in sections	Manageable and clear process	Write in sections	Clear, organised draft
Review	Peer review, self-review, professional edit	Reliable feedback	Peer review	Constructive feedback

Mindfulness and Relaxation Techniques: Incorporating practices to reduce stress and improve emotional regulation.

Example: Mark experiences a lot of stress at work.
Technique: Mindfulness Meditation

Practice Mindfulness: Mark practices mindfulness meditation for 10 minutes each morning.

Body Scan: He performs a body scan to relax and release tension.

Deep Breathing: He uses deep breathing exercises during stressful moments.

Illustration: Mark's mindfulness routine.

Time	Activity	Description
Morning	Mindfulness Meditation	Focus on breath, observe thoughts without judgment
Afternoon	Body Scan	Scan body for tension, release each area
Stressful Moment	Deep Breathing	Inhale deeply for 4 seconds, hold for 4, exhale for 4

Integrating CBT into Daily Life
To effectively integrate CBT techniques into daily life, consistency and practice are crucial. Here are some tips:

Daily Reflection: Spend a few minutes each day reflecting on your thoughts, emotions, and behaviours. Use a journal to document and analyse.

Regular Practice: Make CBT techniques a regular part of your routine and schedule time for mindfulness meditation or cognitive restructuring exercises.

Seek Support: Engage with a therapist or support group to help guide and reinforce your practice.

Be Patient: Recognise that change takes time. Celebrate small victories and stick to the process.

These practical CBT techniques, can help you cultivate a more positive and resilient mindset, better manage stress and anxiety, and improve your overall well-being. The illustrations provided offer a clear framework for implementing these strategies, empowering you to make meaningful changes in your life and achieve your goals in every area of your life.

31

Finding Meaning and Purpose

Find Meaning and Purpose

Embarking on the quest to find meaning and purpose is a deeply personal and transformative journey that has the potential to profoundly enrich your life and enhance your sense of satisfaction. This journey involves more than simply identifying goals or ambitions; it requires delving deep into your core values, passions, and aspirations to discover what truly gives your life significance.

Finding meaning and purpose is not a one-size-fits-all endeavour. Each person's journey is unique, shaped by their individual experiences, beliefs, and desires. It involves a continuous process of self-discovery, reflection, and growth, where you explore what matters most to you and how you can contribute to the world in a way that resonates with your inner self. This journey can lead to greater clarity, motivation, and a more profound connection to life.

In this chapter, we will explore various strategies to help you uncover and cultivate your sense of meaning and purpose. These strategies include introspective exercises, practical examples, and actionable steps to guide you along the way. Whether you are seeking to make a significant life change or simply wanting to deepen your current sense of purpose, these tools can help you navigate your path with confidence and clarity. This chapter aims to provide you with the insights and resources needed to create a life that is not only successful but also deeply fulfilling and aligned with your true self. Embrace this journey with an open heart and mind and discover the profound impact that finding your purpose can have on your overall well-being.

Reflect on Core Values

Strategy
Take time to identify and reflect on your core values—the principles and beliefs that are most important to you. Consider what truly matters to you in life, such as relationships, personal growth, contribution to others, or creativity. Aligning your actions with your values can provide a sense of purpose and direction.

Practical Example
Create a list of your top five values. For instance, if kindness, integrity, and personal growth are high on your list, reflect on how your daily actions and choices align with these values. If personal growth is a value, you might decide to read a new book each month or take a course to develop a new skill. Reflect on moments when you felt happiest or most satisfied and analyse how these moments align with your values.

Explore Interests and Passions

Strategy
Engage in activities that ignite your curiosity and passion. Explore new hobbies, interests, or creative pursuits that bring you joy and fulfilment. Pay attention to activities that energise

and inspire you, as they can provide valuable clues about your true passions and purpose.

Practical Example
If you've always been curious about painting, sign up for a local art class. As you engage in this new hobby, notice how it makes you feel. If it brings you joy and a sense of accomplishment, it could be an indication that your passion lies in creative expression. Alternatively, if you're passionate about animals, consider volunteering at an animal shelter to see if working with animals brings you fulfilment.

Set Meaningful Goals

Strategy
Establish goals that are aligned with your values and aspirations. Whether they are related to your career, relationships, personal growth, or contributing to others, set goals that inspire and motivate you to act. Having clear objectives can give your life direction and purpose, providing a sense of fulfilment as you work towards achieving them.

Practical Example
If one of your values is making a difference in others' lives, set a goal to volunteer at a local shelter once a week. This way, you are not only helping those in need but also aligning your actions with your core values, thereby finding deeper meaning in your life. If personal development is a key value,

you might set a goal to complete a certification course in a field that excites you and is relevant to your progress.

Live for Something Bigger Than Yourself

Strategy
Volunteer your time and skills to help others in need. Giving back to your community or supporting causes you believe in can foster a sense of connection, empathy, and purpose. Acts of kindness and service not only benefit others but also cultivate feelings of fulfilment and meaning in your own life.

Practical Example
Join a local community service group or an organisation like Habitat for Humanity. By building homes for those in need, you directly contribute to improving someone's life, which in turn enriches your sense of purpose and connection to the community. Engage in mentorship programs, where you can offer guidance and support to younger individuals in your field of endeavour or expertise.

Build Meaningful Connections

Strategy
Build meaningful connections with friends, family, and community members who share your values and aspirations. Surround yourself with supportive individuals who inspire and encourage you to pursue your passions and live

authentically. Meaningful relationships provide a sense of belonging and purpose, enriching your life in profound ways.

Practical Example
If you value environmental sustainability, join a local environmental group. Not only will you work towards a cause you believe in, but you will also meet like-minded individuals who can support and inspire you in your journey. Attend networking events and join online communities related to your interests to build a supportive network.

Find Meaning in Challenges

Strategy
Embrace challenges and setbacks as opportunities for growth and self-discovery. Reflect on difficult experiences and consider what lessons they may hold for you. Adversity can often serve as a catalyst for personal transformation and can lead to profound insights about your values, priorities, and purpose.

Practical Example
If you lose your job, rather than seeing it solely as a setback, view it as an opportunity to reassess your career path. Perhaps it's the perfect time to pursue a field that truly excites you or to start your own business. Reflecting on this challenge can reveal new directions and purposes. Use journaling to explore what you've learned from past challenges and how they have shaped your current values and goals.

Cultivate Gratitude

Strategy
Cultivate gratitude for the blessings and opportunities in your life, no matter how small. Take time each day to acknowledge and appreciate the people, experiences, and resources that bring joy and meaning into your life. Cultivating a mindset of gratitude can shift your perspective and enhance your sense of purpose and well-being.

Practical Example
Start a gratitude journal. Each evening, write down three things you are grateful for. This practice can help you focus on the positive aspects of your life and reinforce what is meaningful and purposeful to you. Additionally, express your gratitude to others, whether through a handwritten note or a simple thank you, to build stronger connections.

Finding Meaning and Purpose in a nutshell
Finding meaning and purpose is an ongoing process of self-discovery and exploration. By aligning with your values, passions, and aspirations, and engaging in activities that bring you joy and fulfilment, you can create a life rich in meaning and purpose. This journey leads to greater fulfilment, happiness, and well-being, enabling you to live a life that truly resonates with your deepest self. To embark on this journey, it's crucial to begin with self-reflection, taking the time to understand what truly matters to you. Identify your core values, those fundamental beliefs that guide your actions and

decisions. Reflect on the moments when you felt most satisfied and fulfilled to uncover these guiding principles. Alongside this, explore your passions, activities and interests that excite and energise you. These are the pursuits that make you lose track of time and fill you with a sense of joy and vitality. Things that you will gladly do without pay.

Once you have a clearer understanding of your values and passions, it's important to define your aspirations. These are your long-term goals and dreams, the milestones you wish to achieve in various areas of your life, such as career, relationships, health, and personal growth. Being specific and concrete in defining these goals helps create a mental blueprint for success, aligning your thoughts, emotions, and actions towards achieving them. Visualising your desired outcomes with vivid detail can amplify your focus and clarity. Engage all your senses to make these mental images as real and immersive as possible. Imagine the sights, sounds, smells, and sensations associated with your success, and allow yourself to fully experience the emotions of accomplishment and fulfilment. This practice not only reinforces your belief in your goals but also programs your subconscious mind to work towards these outcomes, enhancing your overall motivation and resolve.

As you progress, stay open to the unexpected. While it's important to have clear goals, flexibility and adaptability are equally crucial. Life is full of surprises, and sometimes, serendipitous events and opportunities can lead you to paths that align even more closely with your true purpose. Embrace these moments with an open heart and mind, allowing them to enrich your journey. Regular practice and commitment to activities that bring you joy, and fulfilment are essential. Incorporate these activities into your daily routine, making them a priority. Whether it's a hobby, a creative pursuit, or spending time with loved ones, these moments of joy enhance your overall well-being, keep you focused, and reinforce your sense of purpose.

The benefits of finding meaning, and purpose are profound. Engaging in meaningful activities boosts your overall happiness and life satisfaction. A strong sense of purpose also enhances your resilience, helping you navigate challenges with a positive outlook. Moreover, when you are passionate about what you do, you are more motivated and engaged, leading to higher productivity and a stronger commitment to your goals. Remember, the quest for meaning and purpose is a continuous journey, one that evolves and deepens over time. As you grow and change, so will your understanding of what gives your life meaning. Regularly reassess your values, passions, and goals, staying curious and open to new experiences and insights. Each step of this journey is valuable and enriching, guiding you towards a life that truly resonates with your deepest self.

32

Support and Connection

Seek Support and Connection

Seeking support and connection is an essential aspect of personal growth, well-being, and resilience. Building meaningful connections with others and reaching out for support during challenging times can provide comfort, validation, and a sense of belonging. Here are some strategies for seeking support and fostering meaningful connections:

Reach Out to Loved Ones
Lean on friends, family members, or trusted individuals in your social circle for emotional support and understanding. Share your thoughts, feelings, and experiences openly and honestly with those you trust, and allow yourself to be vulnerable. Connecting with loved ones can provide comfort, empathy, and a sense of validation, strengthening your bonds and enhancing your well-being.

Join a Support Group
Seek out support groups or community organisations that cater to your specific needs or challenges. Whether you're dealing with mental health issues, addiction recovery, chronic illness, or life transitions, support groups offer a safe and non-judgmental space to share experiences, gain insight, and receive encouragement from others who can relate to your struggles. Connecting with individuals who share similar experiences can foster a sense of solidarity and empowerment.

Consider Therapy or Counselling

If you're struggling with emotional distress, mental health issues, or interpersonal challenges, consider seeking professional help from a therapist or counsellor. Therapy provides a confidential and supportive environment to explore your thoughts, feelings, and behaviours, gain insight into underlying issues, and develop coping strategies to navigate life's challenges. A trained therapist can offer guidance, validation, and personalised support tailored to your unique needs and circumstances.

Volunteer or Get Involved

Engage in volunteer work or community service activities that align with your interests and values. Volunteering not only allows you to make a positive impact in your community but also provides opportunities to connect with like-minded individuals who share your passion for social change and advocacy. Getting involved in meaningful causes can foster a sense of purpose, belonging, and connection with others who share your values and aspirations.

Attend Social Events

Participate in social events, gatherings, or group activities that offer opportunities to meet new people and expand your social network. Whether it's joining a club, attending workshops, or participating in community events, stepping outside your comfort zone and engaging with others can lead to new friendships, connections, and opportunities for personal growth. Be open to meeting people from diverse backgrounds and perspectives and embrace the richness of human interaction.

Be a Supportive Listener
Offer support and compassion to others who may be struggling or in need of a listening ear. Practice active listening skills, empathy, and non-judgmental acceptance when engaging in conversations with friends, family members, or acquaintances who are going through difficult times. Sometimes, simply being present and offering a supportive presence can make a meaningful difference in someone's life. Remember that reaching out for help is a sign of strength, not weakness, and that there are people and resources available to support you on your journey toward personal growth and healing.

33

Progress instead of Perfection

Progress instead of perfection

Shifting your focus from perfectionism to progress is a transformative change in mindset that can significantly enhance your life. This approach emphasises the value of small steps and victories, fostering a sense of accomplishment and continuous improvement. Understand that personal growth is a journey, not a destination, this knowing will help you celebrate your progress, resilience, and commitment to self-improvement. This chapter looks into practical strategies for seeking progress over perfection and explores how to cultivate a mindset of resilience, gratitude, and self-compassion.

Embrace the Progress Mindset

The Essence of Progress Over Perfection
Perfectionism often leads to unrealistic expectations and unnecessary stress. In contrast, a progress-oriented mindset focuses on continual improvement and the journey of personal growth. This shift in perspective allows you to appreciate the value of small, incremental changes rather than striving for an unattainable ideal.

Practical Example
Consider the process of learning a new language. Instead of aiming to speak fluently immediately, set smaller, manageable goals such as learning ten new words each week. Celebrate each new word added to your vocabulary. This

approach not only makes the learning process more enjoyable but also helps you stay motivated by recognising your ongoing progress.

Celebrate Small Victories

The Power of Acknowledgment
Celebrating small victories is crucial for maintaining motivation and reinforcing positive behaviour. Each achievement, no matter how minor, deserves recognition and celebration. This practice not only boosts your confidence but also creates a positive feedback loop that encourages further progress.

Practical Example
If your goal is to improve your physical fitness, start by setting achievable milestones like completing a 10-minute workout three times a week. Celebrate each workout completed, perhaps with a healthy treat or a relaxing activity you enjoy. Over time, gradually increase the duration and intensity of your workouts, celebrating each new milestone reached.

Treat Setbacks as Learning Opportunities

Redefining Setbacks
Setbacks are an inevitable part of any growth journey. Rather than viewing them as failures, see them as opportunities for learning and personal development. Reflect on what went

wrong, identify the lessons learned, and use this knowledge to adjust your approach and move forward with greater insight.

Practical Example
Suppose you are preparing for a major presentation at work, and it doesn't go as planned. Instead of considering it a failure, analyse what happened. Perhaps you discover that you need to improve your public speaking skills or manage your time more effectively. Use these insights to prepare better for future presentations and celebrate the improvements you make along the way.

Cultivate Resilience

Building Mental Toughness
Resilience is the ability to bounce back from setbacks and continue moving forward. Developing resilience involves maintaining a positive outlook, being adaptable, and using adversity as a catalyst for growth. By building resilience, you can navigate life's challenges with greater strength and grace.

Practical Example
If you experience a personal setback, such as a relationship ending, use it as an opportunity to build resilience. Reflect on what you learned from the experience and how it can help you grow. Focus on self-care and personal development and surround yourself with supportive friends and activities that bring you joy.

Practice Self-Compassion

The Role of Kindness
Self-compassion involves treating yourself with the same kindness and understanding you would offer a friend facing similar challenges. This means acknowledging your imperfections, embracing your humanity, and being gentle with yourself in moments of struggle or failure.

Practical Example
When you miss a deadline at work, instead of harshly criticising yourself, practice self-compassion. Recognise that everyone makes mistakes and that it's an opportunity to learn. Reflect on what led to the missed deadline and how you can improve your time management skills in the future. Offer yourself words of encouragement and understanding.

Adopt a Growth Mindset

Embracing Potential
A growth mindset, as described by psychologist Carol Dweck, is the belief that abilities and intelligence can be developed through dedication and hard work. This mindset fosters a love for learning and resilience, essential for achieving great accomplishments.

Practical Example
If you're struggling to learn a new skill, such as playing a musical instrument, adopt a growth mindset by viewing

challenges as opportunities to improve. Instead of saying, "I'm not good at this," reframe your thoughts to, "I'm improving and will get better with practice." Celebrate each new technique or song you learn, and view mistakes as part of the learning process. Show me a person who has never failed, and I will show you a person who has never tried anything in life. Some of the most successful people, have recorded the largest failures before making it.

Set Incremental Goals

Breaking Down Big Goals
Breaking down larger goals into smaller, more manageable tasks makes the journey toward your objectives less daunting and more achievable. Set incremental goals that lead up to your larger aspirations and celebrate each milestone.

Practical Example
If your goal is to write a book, set incremental goals such as writing a chapter each month. Celebrate the completion of each chapter as a significant milestone. This approach makes the larger goal feel more attainable and keeps you motivated.

Create a Supportive Environment

The Importance of Community
Surrounding yourself with supportive individuals who encourage your progress and celebrate your achievements can make a significant difference in maintaining motivation and

resilience. Seek out a community or network of like-minded people who share your goals and values.

Practical Example
Join a support group or online community related to your goals, whether it's a fitness group, a writing club, or a professional network. Share your progress, celebrate each other's achievements, and offer support during setbacks. A supportive environment fosters a sense of belonging and motivation.

Practice Gratitude

Shifting Perspective
Cultivating gratitude involves regularly acknowledging and appreciating the positive aspects of your life. Practicing gratitude can shift your focus from what you lack to what you have, enhancing your sense of purpose and well-being.

Practical Example
Keep a gratitude journal where you write down three things you're grateful for each day. This practice helps you focus on the positive aspects of your life, fostering a sense of contentment and appreciation. Over time, you'll notice a more optimistic outlook and greater resilience in the face of challenges.

Shifting your focus from perfectionism to progress is a transformative mindset change that can profoundly impact your life. This approach encourages you to celebrate small victories, view setbacks as valuable learning opportunities, and cultivate resilience. Practicing self-compassion, adopting a growth mindset, setting incremental goals, creating a supportive environment, and embracing gratitude, will aid you in your navigation of life's challenges with greater grace and adaptability. Remember, personal growth is a continuous journey rather than a fixed destination. Each step forward, no matter how small, is significant and brings you closer to your goals and aspirations. Celebrating your progress, no matter how modest, reinforces positive behaviour and builds momentum. It helps you stay motivated and committed to your path of self-improvement.

Embrace the ups and downs of life with courage and resilience, understanding that setbacks are an integral part of growth. They provide valuable lessons and opportunities to develop strength and perseverance. By shifting your focus to progress, you liberate yourself from the paralysing grip of perfectionism and open to a more fulfilling and enriched existence. Stay committed to your journey of self-discovery and improvement. Celebrate each achievement, learn from every challenge, and continue to move forward with determination and optimism. In doing so, you not only enhance your own life but also inspire those around you to adopt a healthier, more resilient approach to personal growth. Remember, the path to progress is one of continuous learning and evolving, and every step you take is a testament to your strength and potential.

34

Overcoming Procrastination

Overcoming Procrastination

Procrastination is a common challenge that can hinder personal and professional growth. It involves delaying or postponing tasks, often leading to stress, missed opportunities, and diminished productivity. Overcoming procrastination is essential for achieving your goals and living a fulfilling life. In this chapter, we will explore strategies to combat procrastination, supported by practical examples and illustrations to help you implement these techniques.

Understanding Procrastination
Procrastination can stem from various factors, including fear of failure, perfectionism, lack of motivation, and poor time management. Identifying the root cause of your procrastination is the first step toward overcoming it.

Common Reasons for Procrastination:

Fear: Avoiding tasks due to fear of failing.
Perfectionism: Delaying tasks because you want them to be perfect.
Lack of Motivation: Feeling uninspired or unmotivated to start a task.
Poor Time Management: Struggling to prioritize and manage time effectively.

Identifying Procrastination Triggers
To overcome procrastination, it's important to identify your triggers. Keep a log to track when and why you procrastinate.

Illustration: Create a procrastination log.

Date	Task Delayed	Reason for Procrastination	Emotional Response	Consequence
09-04-2024	Writing a report	Fear of not meeting expectations	Anxiety	Missed deadline
10-06-2024	Cleaning the house	Feeling overwhelmed by the task	Stress	Cluttered environment

Strategies to Overcome Procrastination

Set Clear Goals and Priorities
Setting clear, achievable goals helps to focus your efforts and reduce procrastination. Break down larger tasks into smaller, manageable steps.

Example:
Goal: Write a 20-page research paper.
Steps:
Research the topic (Day 1-2)
Create an outline (Day 3)
Write the introduction (Day 4)
Complete the first draft (Day 5-10)

Edit and revise (Day 11-14)

Use Time Management Techniques
Effective time management is crucial for overcoming procrastination. Techniques such as the Pomodoro Technique and time blocking can help manage your time more effectively.

Pomodoro Technique:
Work for 25 minutes, then take a 5-minute break.
After four cycles, take a longer break (15-30 minutes).

Illustration - Pomodoro Technique Cycle:

Work Duration	Break Duration
25 minutes	5 minutes
25 minutes	5 minutes
25 minutes	5 minutes
25 minutes	15-30 minutes

Time Blocking:
Allocate specific blocks of time for different tasks.

Example:
9:00 AM - 10:00 AM: Respond to emails
10:00 AM - 12:00 PM: Work on project A
1:00 PM - 2:00 PM: Attend meetings
2:00 PM - 4:00 PM: Work on project B

Illustration: Time blocking schedule.

Implement the Two-Minute Rule
If a task takes less than two minutes to complete, do it immediately. This helps to quickly clear small tasks, reducing the overall workload.

Example:
Task: Responding to a quick email.
Action: Take two minutes to reply immediately rather than postponing it.

Create a Productive Environment
Your environment can significantly impact your productivity. Ensure your workspace is organized and free from distractions.

Example:
Remove clutter from your desk.
Use noise-cancelling headphones to block out background noise.
Keep essential supplies within reach.

Illustration: Before and after workspace organisation.

Before: Cluttered Desk:
- Papers scattered
- Supplies disorganised
- Distracting items

After: Organised Desk:
- Papers filed
- Supplies in order
- Clean and clear

Practice Self-Compassion
Be kind to yourself when you procrastinate. Understand that everyone experiences procrastination and that it's part of the human experience. Use self-compassion to overcome feelings of guilt and move forward.

Example:
Instead of saying, "I always procrastinate and fail," reframe it as, "I sometimes procrastinate, but I'm working on improving my habits."

Seek Accountability
Having someone to hold you accountable can motivate you to stay on track. This could be a friend, family member, or mentor.

Example:
Share your goals with a friend and schedule regular check-ins to discuss your progress.

One of the most effective tools that I personally use to overcome procrastination is a priority too called, 'The Eisenhower Matrix', which helps separate urgent from nonurgent items and increase productivity and time-resource utilisation.

The Eisenhower Matrix for Prioritising

The Eisenhower Matrix, also known as the Urgent-Important Matrix, is a powerful tool for prioritising tasks and managing time effectively. It helps you distinguish between what needs immediate attention and what can be scheduled for later, delegated, or even eliminated. This chapter will explain the Eisenhower Matrix, provide practical illustrations, and include clear diagrams to help you implement this strategy in your daily life.

Understanding the Eisenhower Matrix

The Eisenhower Matrix divides tasks into four quadrants based on their urgency and importance:

1. **Quadrant I: Urgent and Important**
    - Tasks that need immediate attention and have significant consequences if not completed.
2. **Quadrant II: Not Urgent but Important**
    - Tasks that are important for long-term goals but do not require immediate action.

3. **Quadrant III: Urgent but Not Important**
    - Tasks that require immediate attention but are not critical to long-term success.

4. **Quadrant IV: Not Urgent and Not Important**

o Tasks that are neither urgent nor important and often serve as distractions.

Diagram of the Eisenhower Matrix

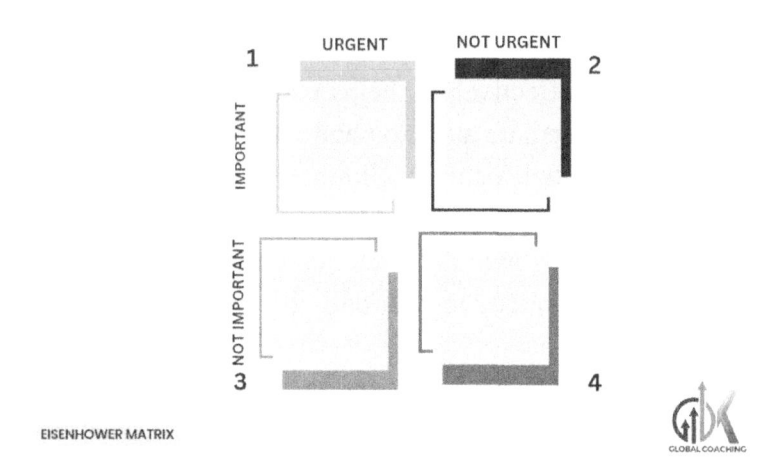

Figure 8: Diagram of the Eisenhower Matrix

Practical Illustrations and Examples
Quadrant I: Urgent and Important
- **Example:** A project deadline is due tomorrow.
  o **Action:** Complete the project immediately.

- **Example:** A critical client call requires immediate response.
  o **Action:** Take the call and address the client's concerns right away.

Quadrant II: Not Urgent but Important
- **Example:** Planning a strategic business proposal.

- **Action:** Schedule dedicated time for in-depth research and preparation.

- **Example:** Regular exercise and health check-ups.
- **Action:** Block time in your calendar for workouts and annual check-ups.

Quadrant III: Urgent but Not Important
- **Example:** Interruptions from co-workers with non-critical questions.
- **Action:** Delegate these queries to a team member or schedule a time to address them.

- **Example:** Attending a routine meeting that does not contribute to your goals.
- **Action:** Delegate the meeting attendance to a subordinate and ask for a summary.

Quadrant IV: Not Urgent and Not Important
- **Example:** Browsing social media aimlessly.
- **Action:** Limit time spent on social media or eliminate it during work hours.

- **Example:** Watching TV shows that do not add value to your life.
- **Action:** Reduce or eliminate watching these shows to free up time for more productivity.

Implementing the Eisenhower Matrix
1. **Identify Tasks:** List all tasks you need to complete.
2. **Categorise Tasks:** Place each task into one of the four quadrants.
3. **Prioritise and Act:** Focus on tasks in Quadrant I first, then plan and work on tasks in Quadrant II. Delegate tasks in Quadrant III and eliminate tasks in Quadrant IV.
4. **Review and Adjust:** Regularly review your matrix to ensure tasks are appropriately categorised and adjust your priorities as needed to eliminate redundant items.

Practical Application
Step-by-Step Example:
1. **List Tasks:**
    - Finish client report (note deadline)
    - Plan next month's marketing strategy
    - Respond to co-worker emails
    - Check social media updates

2. **Categorise Tasks:**
    - **Quadrant I:** Finish client report
    - **Quadrant II:** Plan next month's marketing strategy
    - **Quadrant III:** Respond to emails
    - **Quadrant IV:** Update social media

3. **Prioritise and Act:**
    - **Quadrant I:** Finish client report (Do it now)
    - **Quadrant II:** Plan marketing strategy (Schedule time)
    - **Quadrant III:** Respond to emails (Delegate if possible)
    - **Quadrant IV:** Check social media (Eliminate)

4. **Review and Adjust:**
    - At the end of the day, review completed tasks and adjust the matrix for the next day's priorities.

Overcoming procrastination is a journey that requires self-awareness, effective strategies, and consistent effort. Setting clear goals, managing your time effectively, creating a conducive environment, practicing self-compassion, utilising priority tools, and seeking accountability, will help you break free from the cycle of procrastination. Remember, progress is more important than perfection. Celebrate your small victories and keep moving forward. Each step you take brings you closer to achieving your goals and realising your full potential.

35

Reframing Fear: *From Threat to Opportunity*

Reframing Fear: From Threat to Opportunity

Reframing fear from a threat to an opportunity is a transformative practice that empowers individuals to cultivate courage, resilience, and growth in the face of adversity. Rather than viewing fear as an insurmountable obstacle or something to be avoided, reframing allows us to harness its energy and leverage it as a catalyst for personal development and positive change. Here are some strategies for reframing fear from threat to opportunity:

Shift Your Perspective

Table: Perspective Shifts

Traditional Perspective	Reframed Perspective
Fear is a sign of weakness	Fear is a natural, normal response to the unknown
Fear should be avoided	Fear signals growth and self-discovery
Fear is an obstacle	Fear is an opportunity

Instead of viewing fear as a sign of weakness or vulnerability, see it as a natural and normal response to the unknown or unfamiliar. Recognise that fear is a signal that you are stepping outside your comfort zone and embarking on a journey of growth and self-discovery. By reframing fear as a natural part of the human experience, you can diminish its power over your thoughts and actions.

Embrace the Learning Process

Embrace fear as an opportunity for learning and self-improvement. Every challenge and obstacle presents an opportunity to gain valuable insights, develop new skills, and cultivate resilience. Instead of avoiding fearful situations, lean into them with curiosity and openness, viewing them as opportunities for growth and personal development.

Cultivate a Growth Mindset

Table: Fixed vs. Growth Mindset

Fixed Mindset	Growth Mindset
Abilities are static	Abilities can be developed
Fear is a permanent limit	Fear is a temporary setback
Avoid challenges	Embrace challenges as opportunities for growth

Adopt a growth mindset, believing that your abilities and intelligence can be developed through effort, practice, and perseverance. View fear as a temporary setback rather than a permanent limitation, and approach challenges with a sense of optimism and resilience. By embracing challenges as opportunities for learning and growth, you can develop greater confidence and resilience in the face of fear.

Embrace Growth Over Perfection

Shift your focus from avoiding fear to embracing growth and progress. Instead of seeking to eliminate fear altogether, concentrate on building your capacity to cope with it and thrive despite it. Celebrate the progress you've made and the lessons you've learned along the way, recognising that each experience of fear is an opportunity for growth and self-discovery. Reframe Fear and see it not as a barrier but as a signpost indicating areas ripe for growth. This shift in perspective transforms fear from a paralysing force into a catalyst for development.

Track Small Wins and take lessons: Regularly acknowledge and celebrate small achievements. Whether it's a minor improvement in a skill or a moment of bravery, each step forward is a victory. Take time to reflect on what each fearful experience has taught you. What did you learn about yourself? How did you grow? This reflection reinforces a growth mindset and highlights the value in each struggle. With every challenge come lessons in life.

Understand the Power of Acceptance
Cultivate mindfulness by bringing non-judgmental awareness to your thoughts, feelings, and bodily sensations. Instead of resisting or avoiding fearful emotions, acknowledge them with acceptance and compassion. By observing your fear with curiosity and openness, you can gain insight into its underlying causes and learn to respond to it in a more skilful and adaptive way. Practice Non-Judgmental

Awareness and engage in mindfulness practices that encourage observing your emotions without labelling them as good or bad. This helps create a space where fear can be examined without added stress. When fear arises, treat yourself with the same kindness and understanding you would offer a friend. This self-compassion reduces the intensity of fear and allows you to deal with it more effectively.

Explore Underlying Causes and Adapt: Use curiosity to explore why you feel afraid. What memories trigger your fear? Understanding these root causes can help you address them more constructively. With greater awareness of your fear's origins, experiment with new ways of responding. Instead of habitual avoidance, try approaches that turn fear into a learning experience.

Understanding the Roots of Fear

Evolutionary Biology
Fear is an evolutionary response designed to protect us from harm. Our ancestors relied on fear to avoid predators and dangerous situations. This fear response is known as the fight-or-flight reaction, triggered by the amygdala in the brain.

Learned Responses
Many fears are learned through personal experiences or societal influences. In most cases, these experiences will have long lasting effects. For instance, a traumatic car

accident can lead to a fear of driving, while cultural messages about failure can contribute to a fear of rejection.

Example: Jane had a bad fall while riding a bike as a child. Now, she avoids biking altogether, fearing another accident.

Table: Learned Responses and Their Triggers

Fear	Trigger	Example
Fear of driving	Car accident	Avoiding driving after a crash
Fear of public speaking	Embarrassment	Shaking voice during a speech
Fear of failure	Societal pressure	Avoiding new challenges

Unconscious Beliefs

Deep-seated beliefs formed in childhood can shape our fears. For example, believing that one is unworthy can lead to fears of rejection.

Example: Tom's parents were highly critical, making him believe he isn't good enough. This belief fuels his fear of failure.

Trauma and Past Experiences

Traumatic events can leave lasting psychological impacts, contributing to phobias. Addressing these traumas is crucial for overcoming related fears.

Example: After experiencing a robbery, Emily developed a fear of leaving her house.

Conditioning and Reinforcement
Fear can be reinforced by avoiding situations that trigger it. This avoidance behaviour strengthens the fear over time.

Example: John avoids elevators after getting stuck in one, reinforcing his claustrophobia.

Cultural and Societal Influences
Societal norms and media can shape our fears. For instance, constant news about crimes can heighten fears of personal safety.

Example: Media coverage of plane crashes has heightened Lisa's fear of flying.

Coping Mechanisms and Avoidance Behaviours
Avoidance behaviours provide temporary relief but reinforce fear. Developing healthy coping strategies can help manage and reduce fear.

Example: Instead of avoiding public speaking, Mark practices relaxation techniques and gradually exposes himself to speaking opportunities.

Table: Coping Mechanisms

Coping Mechanism	Description	Example
Mindfulness	Staying present and aware	Meditating before a speech
Relaxation techniques	Breathing exercises to calm nerves	Deep breathing before an exam
Cognitive-behavioural strategies	Challenging negative thoughts	Reframing thoughts about failure

Practical Applications of Cognitive-Behavioural Techniques

Step 1: Identify and Challenge Negative Thoughts

Technique: Cognitive Restructuring
Identify Negative Thoughts: Recognise the irrational thoughts driving your fear.
Challenge These Thoughts: Evaluate their validity and consider alternative perspectives.
Replace with Balanced Thoughts: Develop healthier, more realistic thoughts.
Example: Sarah fears she will fail her presentation. She identifies the thought "I will fail" and challenges it by listing past successes. She replaces it with "I have prepared well and can succeed."

Illustration: Thought record worksheet.

Situation	Automatic Thought	Emotion	Evidence Against Thought	Alternative Thought
Presentation at work	"I will fail"	Anxiety (8/10)	"I have presented successfully before"	"I am well-prepared and capable"

Step 2: Gradual Exposure to Feared Situations

Technique: Exposure Therapy

Create a Fear Hierarchy: List feared situations from least to most anxiety-provoking.

Gradual Exposure: Start with the least feared situation and gradually expose yourself to more challenging situations.

Example: John fears heights. He creates a hierarchy and gradually exposes himself to higher places.

Table: John's Fear Hierarchy

Fear Level	Situation	Anxiety Level (1-10)
1	Standing on a stool	2
2	Climbing a ladder	4
3	Standing on a balcony	6
4	Visiting a tall building's roof	8
5	Skydiving	10

Step 3: Develop Healthy Coping Mechanisms

Technique: Mindfulness and Relaxation
Practice Mindfulness: Focus on the present moment to reduce anxiety.
Use Relaxation Techniques: Engage in deep breathing or progressive muscle relaxation to calm your mind and body.
Example: Before facing a feared situation, Emily practices deep breathing to reduce her anxiety.
Illustration: Deep breathing technique.

Deep Breathing Technique Diagram

Step 1: Find a Comfortable Position
- Sit or lie down in a comfortable position with your back straight.
- Relax your shoulders and place your hands on your lap or by your sides.

Step 2: Inhale Deeply
- Breathe in slowly through your nose for a count of four.
- Focus on filling your abdomen with air first, then your chest. Your abdomen should rise more than your chest.

Step 3: Hold Your Breath
- Hold your breath for a count of four. This helps oxygenate your blood and gives your body a moment to absorb the breath.

Step 4: Exhale Slowly
- Exhale slowly through your mouth for a count of four.
- Purse your lips as if you are blowing out a candle to help control the flow of your breath.

Step 5: Repeat
- Repeat this cycle for 5-10 minutes, focusing on your breath and letting go of any distracting thoughts.

Step 4: Seek Professional Help

Technique: Therapy and Counselling
Cognitive-Behavioural Therapy: Work with a therapist to address irrational thoughts and behaviours.
Support Groups: Join groups where you can share experiences and solutions with others facing the same.
Example: Tom seeks a therapist to help him overcome his fear of failure through structured CBT.

Integrating CBT Techniques into Daily Life
To effectively overcome phobias, consistency and practice are crucial. Here are some tips:

Daily Reflection: Spend a few minutes each day reflecting on your thoughts, emotions, and behaviours. Use a journal to document for analysis.

Regular Practice: Make CBT techniques a regular part of your routine. For example, schedule time for mindfulness meditation or cognitive restructuring.

Seek Support: Engage with a therapist or support group to help guide and reinforce your practice.

Be Patient: Recognise that change takes time. Celebrate small victories and stick to the process.

Reframing Fear as an Opportunity

Instead of seeing fear as a sign of weakness, reframe it as an opportunity to demonstrate courage and resilience. Recognise that true courage is not the absence of fear, but the willingness to confront and overcome it in pursuit of your goals and values. By reframing fear as an opportunity to demonstrate courage and resilience, you can empower yourself to take bold and decisive action in the face of uncertainty. By reframing fear from threat to opportunity, you can cultivate courage, resilience, and growth in the face of adversity. By embracing fear as a natural and normal part of the human experience, you can harness its energy and use it as a catalyst for personal development and positive change. With practice and persistence, you can transform fear from a barrier to a stepping stone on your journey toward greater fulfilment and success.

36

Mental Health Wellbeing

Nurturing Mental Health Wellbeing

In the journey of transformational thinking, nurturing mental health wellbeing stands as a cornerstone for personal growth and fulfilment. Our mental health encompasses our emotional, psychological, and social well-being, influencing how we think, feel, and act in our daily lives. In this chapter, we look into the importance of prioritising mental health and explore practical strategies to foster resilience, emotional balance, and inner peace.

Understanding Mental Health
Mental health is not simply the absence of mental illness but rather a state of overall well-being. It encompasses our ability to cope with stress, maintain healthy relationships, and navigate life's challenges with resilience and grace. However, societal stigmas and misconceptions often prevent individuals from seeking support and addressing their mental health needs. Understanding that mental health is a continuum, ranging from thriving to struggling, will help you create a culture of acceptance and support where you feel empowered to prioritise your mental health and well-being.

The Mind-Body Connection
The mind and body are intricately connected, with each influencing the other in profound ways. Our thoughts and emotions can impact our physical health, while our physical well-being can affect our mental state. By cultivating practices that promote holistic wellness, such as regular

exercise, healthy eating, and adequate sleep, we nourish both our bodies and minds, laying the foundation for optimal mental health.

Building Resilience
Resilience is the ability to bounce back from adversity and thrive in the face of challenges. It is a skill that can be cultivated through self-awareness, positive coping strategies, and a growth mindset. By reframing setbacks as opportunities for growth, practicing self-compassion, and developing effective problem-solving skills, we can strengthen our resilience muscle and navigate life's ups and downs with greater ease and confidence.

Embracing Emotional Intelligence
Emotional intelligence is the ability to recognise, understand, and manage our own emotions, as well as empathise with the emotions of others. By cultivating emotional intelligence, we enhance our self-awareness, interpersonal relationships, and decision-making abilities. Through practices such as mindfulness, journaling, and active listening, we deepen our emotional literacy and foster deeper connections with ourselves and those around us.

Seeking Support and Connection
No journey towards mental health wellbeing is meant to be travelled alone. It is essential to reach out for support and connection during times of need. Whether through therapy, support groups, or trusted friends and family, seeking support

allows us to share our burdens, gain new perspectives, and receive validation and encouragement. By building a support network of individuals who uplift and empower us, we create a safety net of care and compassion to lean on during life's challenges.

Practicing Self-Care
Self-care is the act of prioritising our own physical, emotional, and mental well-being. It involves setting boundaries, practicing self-compassion, and engaging in activities that nourish and rejuvenate us. Whether it's spending time in nature, indulging in a creative hobby, or simply taking a moment to breathe deeply, self-care is an essential practice for replenishing our energy reserves and cultivating a sense of balance and harmony in our lives.

Emergency Mental Health Challenges

Addressing emergency mental health challenges is crucial in ensuring timely intervention and support for individuals experiencing acute psychological distress. These challenges can include conditions such as depression, stress, panic attacks, outbursts of anger, and other urgent mental health issues. Understanding these conditions and knowing how to respond effectively can make a significant difference in managing these emergencies and providing the needed care.

Depression
Depression is a pervasive mental health condition characterised by persistent sadness, loss of interest or pleasure, and a range of physical and emotional problems. When depression becomes severe, it can lead to suicidal ideation or attempts, necessitating immediate intervention.

Practical Example: Jane, a 35-year-old professional, has been struggling with severe depression for months. She isolates herself, loses interest in activities she once enjoyed, and begins to have suicidal thoughts. Recognising the emergency, her friend contacts a mental health crisis hotline, and Jane is quickly connected with a crisis intervention team. She is provided with immediate counselling and a safety plan, and arrangements are made for her to see a psychiatrist for ongoing treatment.

Stress
Stress is the body's response to any demand or challenge. While some stress can be beneficial, chronic or intense stress can lead to severe physical and mental health problems, including anxiety, depression, and burnout.

Practical Example: Tom, a 40-year-old manager, faces extreme stress at work due to an upcoming project deadline. He experiences severe headaches, insomnia, and heightened anxiety. Recognising these as signs of acute stress, Tom's supervisor intervenes by temporarily redistributing his workload and arranging for Tom to meet with the company's employee Mental Wellbeing counsellor. Through stress management techniques and regular counselling, Tom learns to manage stress better.

Panic Attacks
Panic attacks are sudden episodes of intense fear or discomfort, often accompanied by physical symptoms such as heart palpitations, shortness of breath, and dizziness. These attacks can be terrifying and may require immediate assistance.

Practical Example: Sara, a 28-year-old student, experiences a sudden panic attack during an exam. She starts hyperventilating, feels dizzy, and thinks she might faint. Her professor quickly recognizes the symptoms and guides Sara to a quiet room. The professor practices deep breathing exercises with her and reassures her until the symptoms subside. Sara is then referred to the campus mental health services for further evaluation and support.

Outbursts of Anger
Outbursts of anger can occur when an individual is overwhelmed by intense emotions and loses control, potentially leading to aggressive behaviour. These outbursts can be harmful to both the individual and others around them.

Practical Example: Mike, a 45-year-old construction worker, has an outburst of anger on the job site, throwing tools and shouting at his colleagues. Recognising the danger, his supervisor intervenes, calmly asking Mike to step away and take deep breaths. The supervisor then arranges a private meeting where they discuss the stressors contributing to Mike's anger. Mike is referred to an anger management program and given time off to address his mental health needs.

Other Emergency Conditions
Other emergency mental health conditions can include severe anxiety, psychotic episodes, and substance abuse crises. Each requires specific interventions tailored to the individual's needs. Understanding and responding to emergency mental health challenges is vital in providing immediate and effective support to those in crisis.

37

Success Through Transformation

Success Through Transformation

Shifting Perspectives to Foster Success
Shifting perspectives is a powerful strategy for fostering success, enabling you to overcome challenges, unlock new opportunities, and achieve your goals with greater clarity and confidence. By reframing your mindset and adopting a more positive and empowering perspective, you can transform obstacles into opportunities and setbacks into stepping stones on your journey to success. Here are some ways to shift perspectives to foster success, illustrated with practical examples and tables.

Focus on Solutions, Not Problems
Strategy: Shift your focus from dwelling on problems to seeking solutions.

Implementation Steps
Identify the Problem: Write down the specific challenge you're facing.

Ask Empowering Questions: Pose questions that steer your mind toward solutions.

Table 1: Problem-Solving Approach

Problem	Negative Focus	Solution-Oriented Focus	Empowering Question
Missed project deadline	"I failed and it's over."	"What steps can I take to catch up?"	"What can I learn from this experience?"
Low sales performance	"I'm not good at selling."	"What new strategies can I try?"	"How can I improve my sales techniques?"
Poor exam results	"I'm not smart enough."	"What study methods work best for me?"	"What can I change about my study routine?"

Strategy: View setbacks as valuable learning opportunities rather than failures.

Implementation Steps:
Acknowledge the Setback: Recognise and accept the setback.

Extract the Lesson: Identify what you can learn from the experience.

Table 2: Setback Reframing

Setback	Initial Reaction	Reframed Perspective	Lesson Learned
Failed job interview	"I'm not good enough."	"I can improve my interview skills."	"I need to prepare better and practice more."
Business venture didn't take off	"I'm a failure."	"This is a learning experience."	"I need to research market demand more thoroughly."
Argument with a friend	"Our friendship is over."	"We can grow from this."	"I need to communicate more effectively."

Challenge Limiting Beliefs
Strategy: Identify and challenge any limiting beliefs that hold you back.

Implementation Steps:
Identify Limiting Beliefs: Notice negative self-talk and inner critic.

Replace with Empowering Beliefs: Use affirmations and positive self-talk.

Table 3: Challenging Limiting Beliefs

Limiting Belief	Negative Self-Talk	Empowering Affirmation
"I'm not capable."	"I can't do this."	"I am capable and resourceful."
"Success is for others, not me."	"I will never be successful."	"I create my own success."
"I always fail."	"I can't get anything right."	"Every failure is a step towards success."

Resilience and Adaptability

Strategy: Develop resilience and adaptability to navigate challenges.

Implementation Steps:

Develop Coping Strategies: Use mindfulness, exercise, and hobbies.

Seek Support: Lean on friends, family, or professionals.

Table 4: Building Resilience

Challenge	Coping Strategy	Support System
High work stress	Mindfulness meditation	Talk to a trusted colleague
Personal loss	Regular exercise	Join a support group
Major life change	Journaling	Seek counselling

Visualise Success
Strategy: Harness the power of visualisation to imagine success.

Implementation Steps:
Create a Clear Mental Image: Visualise achieving your goals.

Engage Your Senses: Make the visualisation vivid and real.

Table 5: Visualisation Techniques

Goal	Visualisation Description	Sensory Engagement
Getting a promotion	See yourself in the new role, interacting confidently	Feel the excitement, hear the congratulations
Running a marathon	Visualise crossing the finish line strong and happy	Hear the cheers, feel the physical effort
Starting a business	Imagine launching successfully and gaining customers	See the thriving business, hear customer feedback

Shifting Perspectives to Foster Success
Shifting perspectives is a powerful strategy for fostering success, enabling you to overcome challenges, unlock new opportunities, and achieve your goals with greater clarity and confidence. By reframing your mindset and adopting a more positive and empowering perspective, you can transform

obstacles into opportunities and setbacks into stepping stones on your journey to success. Here are some ways to shift perspectives to foster success:

Focus on Solutions, Not Problems
Shift your focus from dwelling on problems to seeking solutions. Instead of getting bogged down by challenges and setbacks, approach them with a solution-oriented mindset. Ask yourself empowering questions such as, "What can I learn from this experience?" and "How can I turn this challenge into an opportunity?" By focusing on solutions, you empower yourself to take proactive steps towards your goals and ultimately, your success.

Reframe Setbacks as Lessons
Instead of viewing setbacks as failures, reframe them as valuable learning opportunities. Embrace the lessons that setbacks offer and use them to inform your future actions and decisions. Adopt a growth mindset, recognising that setbacks are not permanent obstacles but temporary detours on the path to your intended and or desired success.

Challenge Limiting Beliefs
Identify and challenge any limiting beliefs that may be holding you back from achieving your full potential. Notice the negative self-talk and inner critic that may undermine your confidence and resilience. Replace limiting beliefs with empowering affirmations and positive self-talk, reinforcing your belief in your ability to succeed.

Be Resilient and Learn to Adapt
Develop resilience and adaptability to navigate challenges and setbacks with grace and perseverance. Recognise that change is inevitable and embrace it as an opportunity for growth and transformation. Cultivate resilience by developing coping strategies, seeking support from others, and maintaining a positive attitude in the face of adversity.

Visualise Success
Harness the power of visualisation to imagine yourself succeeding in your endeavours. Create a clear mental image of your goals and visualise yourself achieving them with confidence and determination. Engage your senses and emotions to make the visualisation as vivid and real as possible, reinforcing your belief in your ability to succeed. With a positive and empowering perspective, you can create the life you desire and thrive in the face of any challenge.

38

Creating New Philosophies and Belief Systems

Create New Philosophies and Belief Systems

Creating new philosophies and belief systems is an empowering journey that enables personal growth and development. By examining existing beliefs, you can identify those that no longer serve you and replace them with empowering beliefs aligned with your goals and values. Here's a structured approach to help you through this process:

Examine Existing Belief Systems

Table: Steps to Examine Existing Belief Systems

Step	Description
Identify Core Beliefs	Recognise fundamental principles shaping your worldview
Challenge Assumptions	Question limiting or outdated beliefs
Examine the Evidence	Seek information that supports or contradicts your beliefs
Practice Curiosity	Approach with openness and willingness to explore
Experiment with New Beliefs	Test new perspectives to see their impact
Embrace Change	Accept growth and evolution in your belief system

1. Identify Core Beliefs

Identify your core beliefs – the fundamental principles and values that shape your worldview and guide your behaviour. These beliefs may have been formed in childhood or influenced by cultural, social, and environmental factors. Pay attention to recurring themes or patterns in your beliefs to gain insight into their origins and impact on your life.

2. Challenge Assumptions

Challenge assumptions and beliefs that may be limiting or outdated. Ask yourself why you believe certain things and whether they are based on evidence or simply inherited from others. Consider alternative perspectives and be open to questioning long-held beliefs that no longer serve your purpose.

3. Examine the Evidence

Examine the evidence that supports or contradicts your beliefs. Seek out information, experiences, and perspectives that challenge your existing beliefs and expand your understanding of the world. Be willing to revise your beliefs considering new evidence or insights that emerge from your exploration.

Table: Evidence Examination

Belief	Supporting Evidence	Contradicting Evidence
Example 1	Evidence A	Evidence X
Example 2	Evidence B	Evidence Y

4. Practice Curiosity and Openness
Approach the process of examining beliefs with curiosity and openness, rather than judgment or defensiveness. Be willing to explore uncomfortable or challenging ideas and embrace the opportunity for growth and self-discovery. Cultivate a mindset of lifelong learning and evolution.

5. Experiment with New Beliefs
Experiment with new beliefs and perspectives to see how they resonate with you and impact your life. Test out affirmations, mantras, or positive statements that align with the beliefs you wish to cultivate. Notice how adopting new beliefs influences your thoughts, feelings, and actions over time.

6. Embrace Change
Embrace the process of growth and change as you examine and evolve your beliefs. Understand that beliefs are not fixed or immutable but can be modified and refined as you gain new insights and life experiences. Be patient and compassionate with yourself as you navigate the journey of self-discovery and transformation.

39

Constructing Empowering Beliefs

Construction Empowering Beliefs

Constructing empowering beliefs is a transformative process that involves intentionally shaping your mindset to support your goals, aspirations, and well-being. By cultivating empowering beliefs, you can enhance your confidence, resilience, and ability to navigate life's challenges with grace and determination. This chapter explores the steps and strategies for constructing empowering beliefs, complete with practical examples to help you integrate these principles into your daily life.

Understanding Empowering Beliefs

The Impact of Empowering Belief
Empowering beliefs are positive and constructive thoughts that reinforce your self-worth, capabilities, and potential. These beliefs shape your perception of yourself and the world, influencing your actions and outcomes. Unlike limiting beliefs, which hinder your progress and create self-doubt, empowering beliefs provide the foundation for growth and resilience. Your beliefs act as a lens through which you view and interpret your experiences. They influence your decisions, behaviours, and emotional responses. Constructing empowering beliefs allows you to approach challenges with a positive mindset and will help you persist in the face of adversity.

Steps for Creating Empowering Beliefs

1. Identify and Challenge Limiting Beliefs
The first step in constructing empowering beliefs is to identify the limiting beliefs that are holding you back and their origins. These are often deeply ingrained and may stem from past experiences, societal conditioning, or negative self-talk.

Practical Example: If you find yourself thinking, "I'm not good enough to achieve my goals," recognise this as a limiting belief. Write it down and examine its origins. Reflect on past experiences or influences that may have contributed to this belief.

Challenge Limiting Beliefs
Once you have identified a limiting belief, challenge its validity. Question whether it is based on facts or assumptions. Look for evidence that contradicts the belief and consider alternative, more positive perspectives.

Practical Example: Challenge the belief "I'm not good enough" by listing your achievements, skills, and positive feedback from others. Remind yourself of times when you succeeded despite initial doubts. Replace the limiting belief with a more empowering one, such as "I have the skills and determination to achieve my goals."

2. Create and Affirm Empowering Beliefs

Define Empowering Beliefs
Empowering beliefs should be specific, positive, and aligned with your values and goals. They should inspire confidence and motivate you to act.

Practical Example: Create an empowering belief such as "I am capable of overcoming challenges and achieving success in my career." Ensure that it resonates with your personal aspirations and values.

Affirm Empowering Beliefs
Affirmations are powerful tools for reinforcing empowering beliefs. Repeatedly stating your empowering beliefs helps to embed them in your subconscious mind, gradually replacing old beliefs.

Practical Example: Start each day by affirming your empowering belief: "I am capable of overcoming challenges and achieving success in my career." Repeat this affirmation multiple times, with conviction, and visualise yourself embodying this belief in real-life situations.

3. Take Action to Reinforce Beliefs

Align Actions with Beliefs
To solidify empowering beliefs, align your actions with them. Consistently acting in ways that reflect your empowering

beliefs helps to reinforce them and build confidence in their truth.

Practical Example: If your empowering belief is "I am capable of overcoming challenges and achieving success in my career," take proactive steps towards your career goals. This could include seeking new opportunities, enhancing your skills through training, or networking with industry professionals.

Celebrate Progress and Learn from Setbacks

Acknowledge and celebrate your progress, no matter how small. Recognise that setbacks are part of the journey and use them as opportunities for growth.

Practical Example: Celebrate achievements such as completing a challenging project or receiving positive feedback. When facing setbacks, reflect on what you can learn from the experience and how you can improve. Reinforce your empowering belief by reminding yourself of your capabilities and resilience.

4. Surround Yourself with Positive Influences

Build a Supportive Network

Surround yourself with individuals who support and encourage your growth. Positive influences can reinforce your empowering beliefs and provide motivation and guidance.

Practical Example: Join a professional group that shares your interests and values. Seek mentors who can offer advice and encouragement. Engage with friends and colleagues who inspire and lift you up.

Limit Exposure to Negative Influences
Minimise interactions with people or environments that reinforce limiting beliefs or negative self-talk. Protecting your mental and emotional well-being is crucial for maintaining empowering beliefs.

Practical Example: Set boundaries to protect yourself from relationships or situations that consistently bring you down. Focus on spending time with positive and encouraging relationships instead.

5. Practice Mindfulness and Self-Reflection

Develop Mindfulness
Mindfulness involves being present in the moment and observing your thoughts and feelings without judgment. Practicing mindfulness helps you become aware of limiting beliefs and allows you to consciously choose empowering thoughts.

Practical Example: Incorporate mindfulness practices such as meditation, deep breathing, or journaling into your daily routine. When you notice negative self-talk or limiting beliefs, pause and reframe your thoughts with empowering beliefs.

Engage in Self-Reflection
Regular self-reflection helps you evaluate your progress and identify areas for improvement. Reflect on your beliefs, actions, and experiences to ensure they align with your empowering beliefs and goals.

Practical Example: At the end of each week, take time to reflect on your achievements, challenges, and growth. Ask yourself questions like, "How did I embody my empowering beliefs this week?" and "What can I learn from my experiences?"

Constructing or creating empowering beliefs is a transformative process that enhances your confidence, resilience, and ability to navigate life's challenges. Embrace this journey of personal growth and empowerment, and remember that every step forward, no matter how small, brings you closer to the life that you seek and desire.

40

Living in Alignment with Personal Values

Living in Alignment with Personal Values

Living in alignment with your personal values is the cornerstone of a fulfilling and authentic life. When your actions, decisions, and behaviours reflect your core principles, you experience a profound sense of congruence, purpose, and satisfaction. This chapter delves into the importance of identifying and embracing your values and offers practical strategies to help you align your daily life with what truly matters to you. By understanding and living according to your personal values, you can navigate life's challenges with greater clarity and resilience, ultimately leading to a more meaningful and enriched existence. Let's explore how to effectively live in alignment with your personal values, and the transformative impact this can have on your overall well-being and happiness.

Identify Your Core Values and Clarify Priorities
Take time to identify your core values – the principles and beliefs that are most important to you. Reflect on what matters deeply to you, what you stand for, and what gives your life meaning and purpose. Your values might include honesty, integrity, compassion, growth, creativity, or connection, among others. Clarify your priorities based on your core values. Determine what aspects of life are most meaningful to you, whether it's relationships, career, health, personal growth, or contribution to society. Prioritise activities and commitments that align with your values and bring you a sense of fulfilment and satisfaction.

Have Integrity and be Authentic

Practice integrity and authenticity in all aspects of your life by staying true to your values, even in challenging situations. Be honest, transparent, and consistent in your actions and interactions with others. Living with integrity fosters trust, respect, and meaningful connections, both within yourself and in your relationships with others. Regularly evaluate how well your life aligns with your values and adjust as needed. Reflect on whether certain areas of your life are congruent with your core principles and identify any areas where you may need to realign your behaviours or priorities. Be willing to make changes that better support your values and lead to greater harmony and fulfilment. Seek support from friends, family members, or mentors who share your values and can provide encouragement and accountability on your journey. Surround yourself with individuals who inspire and empower you to live in alignment with your values and be open to receiving feedback and guidance as you navigate your path. Embrace your values as guiding principles that shape your choices and actions and allow them to lead you towards a life of purpose, joy, and integrity.

Align Your Actions with Your Values

Align your daily actions and behaviours with your values. Make conscious choices that honour your core principles and contribute to your overall well-being and happiness. Consider how your actions impact yourself and others, and strive to act with integrity, authenticity, and compassion in all areas of your life. Set goals and aspirations that are aligned with your core values. Define what success means to you based on your values rather than external standards or societal expectations. Set meaningful objectives that resonate with your authentic self and contribute to your sense of purpose and fulfilment. Make decisions based on your values rather than external pressures or desires for approval. When faced with choices or dilemmas, consider how each option aligns with your core principles and which course of action feels most authentic and true to yourself. Trust your intuition and inner wisdom to guide you towards decisions that honour your values and lead to greater fulfilment.

Benefits of Alignment

1. Enhanced Productivity
When your daily routines are aligned with your personal goals, you focus your energy and resources on activities that matter most. This prioritisation helps eliminate distractions and reduces time spent on less important tasks, thereby boosting your productivity.

Example: If your personal goal is to improve your physical fitness, incorporating a morning workout routine ensures that you consistently make progress towards this goal.

2. Increased Motivation
Seeing how your daily efforts contribute to your larger objectives can significantly boost your motivation. This connection between routine actions and long-term

achievements creates a sense of accomplishment and drives you to stay committed to your goals.

Example: If you aim to write a book, dedicating a specific time each day to writing can keep you motivated as you see the pages accumulate over time.

3. Greater Consistency
Consistency is key to achieving any goal. By embedding goal-oriented activities into your daily routine, you create habits that support sustained progress. This regularity ensures that you are continually moving towards your goals, even on days when motivation wanes.

Example: If your goal is to learn a new language, setting aside 30 minutes each day for language practice can help build and reinforce your skills consistently.

4. Improved Time Management
Aligning your routines with your goals helps you manage your time more effectively. You become more intentional with your schedule, ensuring that your time is spent on activities that advance your personal and professional objectives.

Example: If advancing your career is a goal, scheduling time each day for professional development activities, such as taking online courses, can help you manage your time effectively.

5. Enhanced Well-being

Achieving personal goals contributes to a sense of fulfilment and happiness. When your daily routines reflect your aspirations, you experience a greater sense of purpose and satisfaction in your life.

Example: If your goal is to cultivate mindfulness, integrating meditation or mindfulness exercises into your daily routine can enhance your overall well-being and reduce stress.

Strategies for Alignment

1. Set Clear and Specific Goals

Define your personal goals clearly and specifically. Break them down into actionable steps that can be incorporated into your daily routine.

Example: Instead of setting a vague goal like "get healthier," specify actions such as "eat a balanced breakfast" or "exercise for 30 minutes daily."

2. Prioritise Your Activities

Identify the most important tasks that align with your goals and prioritise them in your daily schedule. Use tools like to-do lists, planners, or digital calendars to keep track of these activities.

Example: If your goal is to advance your career, prioritise tasks such as networking, skill development, or project completion in your daily agenda.

3. Create a Structured Routine
Design a structured daily routine that incorporates goal-oriented activities at specific times. Consistency in scheduling helps build habits and ensures that these activities become an integral part of your day.

Example: If your goal is to write a book, allocate a specific time each day, such as early morning or late evening, for writing sessions.

4. Track Your Progress
Regularly monitor your progress towards your goals. Tracking helps you stay accountable and allows you to celebrate milestones along the way, reinforcing your commitment to your routines.

Example: Use a journal or an app to log daily achievements related to your goals, such as workout sessions, completed chapters, or piano practice hours.

5. Stay Flexible and Adjust
While consistency is important, it's also crucial to remain flexible and adjust your routines as needed. Life circumstances may change, and being adaptable ensures that you continue to progress towards your goals without becoming discouraged.

Example: If a busy work schedule disrupts your exercise routine, find alternative times or shorter workouts to stay on track.

Aligning your daily routines with your personal goals is a powerful way to enhance productivity, motivation, consistency, time management, and overall well-being. This strategic alignment helps ensure that every action you take is purposeful and directed towards achieving your long-term aspirations. By setting clear goals, you create a roadmap for your success. Clear goals provide a sense of direction and purpose, enabling you to focus your efforts on what truly matters. This focus is crucial for productivity, as it minimises distractions and ensures that your energy is invested in productive activities.

Prioritising activities is another key aspect of this alignment. When you prioritise, you identify the tasks that have the greatest impact on your goals and allocate your time and resources accordingly. This not only boosts your efficiency but also keeps you motivated, as you see tangible progress towards your objectives. Creating structured routines further supports this process. A well-defined routine establishes a consistent framework for your daily activities, reducing decision fatigue and helping you build momentum. Consistency is a critical component of success; by making goal-oriented actions a regular part of your routine, you cultivate habits that propel you steadily towards your aspirations.

Tracking progress is essential for maintaining momentum and staying on course. By regularly reviewing your achievements and setbacks, you gain valuable insights into what works and what needs adjustment. This feedback loop enhances your ability to manage your time effectively, ensuring that you remain adaptable and responsive to changing circumstances. Staying flexible is equally important. While structure and consistency are vital, life is unpredictable, and rigid adherence to a plan can sometimes be counterproductive. Flexibility allows you to adjust your routines and goals in response to new opportunities and challenges, maintaining a dynamic balance between stability and adaptability.

Incorporating these elements into your daily life not only brings you closer to achieving your goals but also enriches your daily experience. When your actions align with your aspirations, each day becomes infused with a sense of purpose and fulfilment. This alignment fosters a deep sense of satisfaction and well-being, as you see the meaningful impact of your efforts unfold over time. In conclusion, the deliberate alignment of your daily routines with your personal goals is a holistic approach that enhances productivity, motivation, consistency, time management, and overall well-being. By setting clear goals, prioritising activities, creating structured routines, tracking progress, and staying flexible, you can create a life that is not only goal-oriented but also deeply rewarding.

41

You are what you think

You Are What You Think

"You are what you think" encapsulates the profound influence of our thoughts on our lives, actions, and experiences. Our mental landscape shapes our beliefs, attitudes, and perceptions of reality, ultimately influencing how we engage with the world and the outcomes we achieve. Understanding the power of our thoughts is crucial for personal growth and transformation. This chapter explores the intricate connection between our mindset and our lived reality, exploring how positive thinking can lead to greater success, while negative thinking can create obstacles and limitations. Harness the power of your thoughts, and reshape our life, overcome challenges, and achieve your highest potential. Let's explore why "you are what you think" holds true and how you can cultivate a mindset that empowers you.

Thoughts Shape Beliefs

Table: Positive vs. Negative Thoughts

Positive Thoughts	Negative Thoughts
"I can achieve my goals."	"I'm not good enough."
"Challenges help me grow."	"Challenges mean failure."
"I am worthy of success."	"Success is out of reach."

Our thoughts form the foundation of our beliefs about ourselves, others, and the world around us. Positive thoughts cultivate empowering beliefs that bolster confidence, resilience, and self-worth, while negative thoughts can foster limiting beliefs that undermine our potential and hold us back.

Mindset Drives Behaviour

Graph: Mindset and Behaviour

Our mindset, or the pattern of our thoughts and beliefs, significantly impacts our behaviour and actions. A positive, growth-oriented mindset leads to proactive behaviours, goal setting, and perseverance in the face of challenges, whereas a negative, fixed mindset can result in self-doubt, avoidance, and self-sabotage.

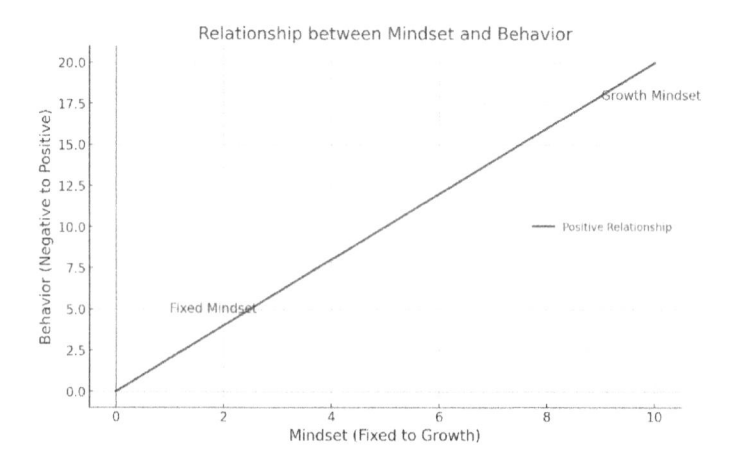

Figure 9: Graph illustrating the relationship between mindset and behaviour

X-axis (Mindset): Represents the continuum from a fixed mindset (left) to a growth mindset (right).

Y-axis (Behaviour): Represents the spectrum from unproductive/negative behaviour (bottom) to productive/positive behaviour (top).

The positive trend line shows that as mindset shifts from fixed to growth, behaviour tends to become more positive and productive. This visual representation highlights how adopting a growth mindset can lead to more constructive and beneficial behaviours.

Thoughts Influence Emotions

Table: Thoughts and Corresponding Emotions

Thought	Emotion
"I am grateful for today."	Joy
"I can handle this."	Confidence
"I always mess up."	Sadness
"Nobody likes me."	Loneliness

Our thoughts have a direct influence on our emotions and mood states. Positive thoughts generate feelings of joy, gratitude, and optimism, while negative thoughts can trigger emotions such as fear, anger, or sadness. By cultivating a positive internal dialogue, we can enhance our emotional well-being.

Self-Talk Shapes Self-Image

Illustration: Positive vs. Negative Self-Talk

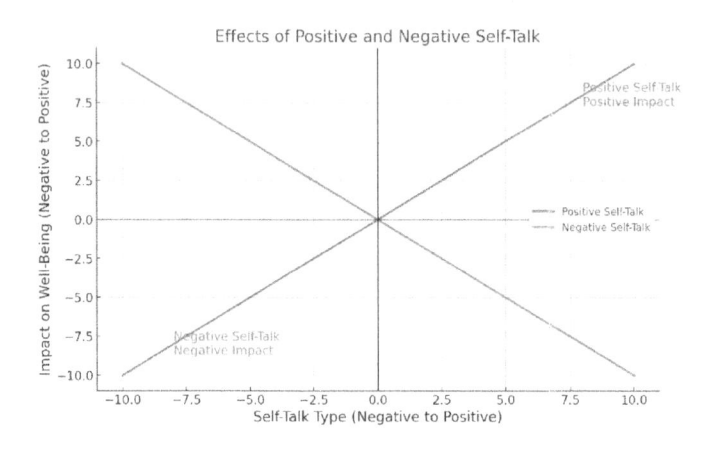

Figure 10: Graph illustrating the effects of positive and negative self-talk

X-axis (Self-Talk Type): Ranges from negative self-talk (left) to positive self-talk (right).

Y-axis (Impact on Well-Being): Measures the impact on well-being, from negative to positive.

The green line *(which starts from 10 to -10)* represents positive self-talk, which is associated with improvements in performance, confidence, reduced stress levels, and overall better mental health. The red line *(which starts from -10 to 10)* represents negative self-talk, which is associated with declines in performance, lower confidence, increased stress levels, and poorer mental health. This visual clearly shows that positive self-talk leads to positive outcomes, while negative self-talk leads to negative outcomes, emphasising the importance of maintaining positive self-talk for overall well-being. The way we talk to ourselves, known as self-talk, plays a crucial role in shaping our self-image and self-esteem. Positive self-talk reinforces a healthy self-concept and fosters self-compassion, while negative self-talk can erode self-confidence and perpetuate feelings of inadequacy.

Thoughts Create Reality

Graph: Perception and Reality

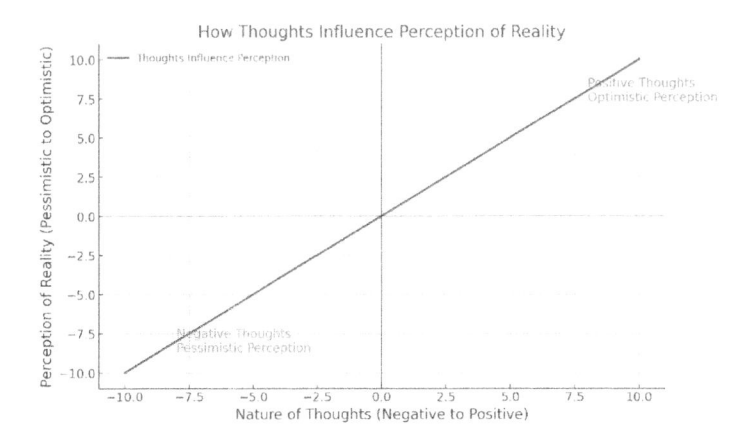

Figure 11: Graph illustrating how thoughts influence our perception of reality

X-axis (Nature of Thoughts): Ranges from negative thoughts (left) to positive thoughts (right).

Y-axis (Perception of Reality): Ranges from pessimistic perception (bottom) to optimistic perception (top).

The blue line represents the direct relationship between the nature of our thoughts and our perception of reality. As thoughts become more positive, perception of reality becomes more optimistic, and as thoughts become more negative, perception of reality becomes more pessimistic. This illustration emphasises the significant impact that our thoughts have on how we perceive and interpret our reality, highlighting the importance of maintaining positive thinking to foster a more optimistic outlook on life.

Focus Determines Direction
Where we choose to focus our thoughts determines the direction of our lives. By directing our attention towards our goals, values, and aspirations, we can channel our energy and efforts into pursuits that align with our deepest desires. Conversely, dwelling on negativity or past failures can impede our progress and hinder our growth.

Thoughts Shape Relationships

Table: Impact of Thoughts on Relationships

Positive Thoughts	Relationship Outcome
"I appreciate you."	Strengthened bond
"I understand your perspective."	Increased empathy
"You never do anything right."	Conflict and tension
"I don't trust anyone."	Disconnection

Our thoughts influence the way we perceive and interact with others, shaping the quality of our relationships. Positive thoughts foster empathy, compassion, and connection, while negative thoughts can lead to judgment, conflict, and disconnection. Cultivating a mindset of understanding and acceptance can enrich our relationships and strengthen social bonds. In essence, "you are what you think" underscores the transformative power of our thoughts in shaping our lives and experiences.

42

Your focus determines your Actions

What you focus on determines your actions

"What you focus on will determine your actions" speaks to the profound influence of our attention on the choices we make and the behaviours we exhibit. Our focus directs our energy and shapes our intentions, guiding us towards specific courses of action. Here's why what you focus on dictates your actions. Wherever we focus our attention, our energy follows. Directing your attention towards specific goals, tasks, or priorities, will have you allocate your mental and emotional resources to those areas, increasing the likelihood of taking action to achieve them.

Clarity Leads to Action
Focusing on clear goals or objectives provides clarity about what needs to be done, motivating us to take action to attain them. When we have a clear vision of what we want to accomplish, we are more likely to develop actionable plans and take steps towards realising our aspirations. Concentrating on what truly matters filters out distractions and irrelevant stimuli, enabling us to maintain focus on our priorities and goals. Our attention shapes our intentions and mindset, influencing the quality of our actions. When we focus on positive outcomes and growth opportunities, our intentions become aligned with our goals, prompting proactive and constructive actions.

Perception Determines Response
How we perceive a situation or circumstance influences our response and subsequent actions. By shifting our focus from obstacles to possibilities, from limitations to opportunities, we adopt a mindset that is conducive to taking proactive and solution-oriented actions. Consistently directing our attention towards specific behaviours or habits reinforces their importance and strengthens our commitment to them. Through focused attention, we can cultivate positive habits and routines that support our goals and aspirations over time.

Attention Fuels Motivation
Focusing on meaningful goals or values fuels our motivation and determination to act. When we are deeply invested in what we are focusing on, we are more likely to overcome obstacles, persist in the face of challenges, and take consistent action towards our objectives. Our mindset, influenced by our focus, drives our behaviour and decision-making process. A growth-oriented focus fosters resilience, adaptability, and a willingness to take risks, leading to actions that facilitate a growth mindset.

Focus Enhances Productivity
Concentrating on specific tasks or objectives enhances productivity by channelling our efforts and resources towards their accomplishment. By focusing on one task at a time, we can avoid overwhelm and make steady progress towards our goals. Ultimately, what we focus on shapes our reality by influencing the actions we take and the outcomes we

experience. What you focus on profoundly influences your actions, decisions, and ultimately, the trajectory of your life. Developing focused attention on what truly matters to you, will empower you to take purposeful action and manifest your intentions into reality.

Embrace Co-Creation and Collaboration
Creating your future is not a solitary endeavour, and embracing co-creation and collaboration with others amplifies your creative power and potential. In essence, creating your future with your mind is a transformative practice that empowers you to become the conscious architect of your destiny. You unlock your innate creative potential by harnessing the power of intention, cultivating a positive mindset, visualising your outcomes, taking inspired action, and trusting the process. "What you focus on determines your actions" underscores the profound influence of our attention on our choices and behaviours. When you direct your focus towards specific goals, tasks, or priorities, you channel your mental and emotional resources effectively, thereby taking decisive action.

Clear goals provide the clarity needed to formulate actionable plans, while minimising distractions creates an environment conducive to productivity. Our focus shapes our intentions and mindset, influencing the quality of our actions and responses. Shifting our perception from obstacles to opportunities promotes proactive and solution-oriented behaviour. Consistently directing attention towards positive habits reinforces their importance and strengthens our commitment. Focusing on meaningful goals fuels motivation and determination, helping us overcome obstacles and persist in the face of challenges. A growth-oriented focus fosters resilience and adaptability, enhancing our decision-making process. When we concentrate on specific tasks, we enhance productivity. Ultimately, what we focus on shapes our reality by guiding our actions and influencing our outcomes. Embracing co-creation and collaboration further amplifies our creative potential, fostering supportive relationships and accelerating progress towards our goals.

43

A Journey to Personal Fulfilment

Embracing Transformational Thinking

A Journey to Personal Fulfilment
Understanding yourself through transformational thinking is a profound journey of self-discovery, growth, and empowerment. It involves harnessing the power of the mind to explore the depths of your consciousness, uncovering hidden truths, and transcending limitations to realise your fullest potential. Here are some key insights into understanding yourself by harnessing the power of your mind through transformational thinking:

Self-Reflection and Awareness
Transformational thinking begins with self-reflection and awareness, inviting individuals to explore their thoughts, emotions, and beliefs with honesty and curiosity. Through introspective practices such as journaling, meditation, and contemplation, individuals gain insight into their inner world, unravelling layers of conditioning and discovering their authentic selves beneath the surface.

Challenging Limiting Beliefs
Transformational thinking involves challenging limiting beliefs and narratives that hinder personal growth and fulfilment. By questioning inherited beliefs, societal norms, and cultural conditioning, individuals free themselves from the constraints of the past, opening new possibilities for self-expression, creativity, and empowerment.

Embracing Vulnerability and Authenticity
Transformational thinking encourages individuals to embrace vulnerability and authenticity as pathways to self-discovery and connection. By courageously revealing their true selves, flaws, and all, individuals cultivate deeper relationships, authenticity, and self-acceptance, fostering a sense of belonging and connection with others.

Healing Past Wounds and Trauma
Transformational thinking provides a framework for healing past wounds and trauma, allowing individuals to release emotional baggage and reclaim their power. Through practices such as forgiveness, self-compassion, and inner child work, individuals heal old wounds, cultivate resilience, and step into their wholeness and sovereignty.

Cultivating Self-Compassion and Love
Transformational thinking fosters self-compassion and love as essential components of personal growth and well-being. By treating oneself with kindness, understanding, and unconditional love, individuals nurture a positive relationship with themselves, fostering inner peace, happiness, and fulfilment.

Aligning with Purpose and Authentic Expression
Transformational thinking guides individuals towards aligning with their purpose and authentic expression in the world. By listening to the whispers of their soul, following their passions, and living in alignment with their values,

individuals find meaning, fulfilment, and joy in their lives, contributing their unique gifts and talents to the world.

Embracing Continuous Growth and Evolution
Transformational thinking is a lifelong journey of growth and evolution, characterised by a commitment to continuous learning, exploration, and self-improvement. By embracing change, uncertainty, and the unknown, individuals expand their horizons, deepen their understanding of themselves and the world, and evolve into their highest potential.

In essence, understanding oneself through transformational thinking is a transformative journey of self-discovery, empowerment, and awakening. By embracing self-reflection, challenging limiting beliefs, and cultivating authenticity, individuals unlock the door to their true essence, reclaiming their power and sovereignty, and living lives of purpose, passion, and fulfilment. In the culmination of our transformative journey, we stand at the threshold of a profound realisation – that true fulfilment lies not in the destination, but in the journey itself. As we reflect on the principles of transformational thinking that have guided us thus far, we recognise that personal fulfilment is not merely a destination to reach, but a way of being to embrace. In this final chapter, we look into the essence of embracing transformational thinking as a lifelong journey towards success.

The Evolution of Self

Transformational thinking invites us to embark on a journey of self-discovery and evolution, where we continuously shed old layers of conditioning and embrace new facets of our authentic selves. As we cultivate self-awareness, we deepen our understanding of who we are and what we value, allowing us to live in alignment with our true essence.

Embracing Growth and Change

Central to transformational thinking is the recognition that growth and change are inherent aspects of the human experience. Rather than fearing the unknown or clinging to the familiar, we learn to embrace change as a catalyst for growth and evolution. When we step out of our comfort zones and embrace new challenges, we expand our horizons and unlock new potentials within ourselves. Living with Purpose and Passion: Transformational thinking calls us to live with purpose and passion, aligning our actions with our deepest values and aspirations. As we clarify our goals and pursue endeavours that resonate with our authentic selves, we infuse our lives with meaning and vitality. Whether it's pursuing our passions, making a difference in the lives of others, or contributing to causes greater than ourselves, we find fulfilment in living in alignment with our purpose.

Cultivating Resilience and Adaptability

In the face of adversity and setbacks, transformational thinking equips us with the resilience and adaptability to navigate life's challenges with grace and courage. Rather than succumbing to fear or despair, we embrace setbacks as opportunities for growth and learning. By harnessing the power of our minds and the resilience of the human spirit, we emerge from adversity stronger, wiser, and more resilient.

Nurturing Connection and Community
Transformational thinking reminds us of the importance of connection and community in our journey towards fulfilment. As social beings, we thrive in the support and companionship of like-minded individuals who uplift and inspire us. By cultivating meaningful relationships and fostering a sense of belonging, we enrich our lives and contribute to the collective well-being of humanity.

Celebrating the Journey
Ultimately, embracing transformational thinking is about celebrating the journey – the highs and lows, the triumphs and challenges, the moments of joy and moments of growth. Each step along the way is a testament to our courage, resilience, and commitment to personal evolution. As we look back on how far we've come, we embrace gratitude for the lessons learned, the growth experienced, and the person we've become. What you are becoming and ultimately become, matters more than the achievements.

Finally, in the tapestry of life, transformational thinking is the thread that weaves together our hopes, dreams, and aspirations into a masterpiece of personal fulfilment. It is a journey of self-discovery, growth, and evolution; a journey that leads us not only to the fulfilment of our individual potential but also to a deeper connection with the world around us. As we embrace transformational thinking as a way of life, we step into our power as creators of our own destiny, architects of our own fulfilment. With each thought, belief, and action, we shape our reality and manifest our deepest desires into being. So, dare to dream, dare to believe, and dare to embrace the transformative power of your own mind, for within you lies the limitless potential to create a life of purpose, passion, and personal fulfilment. Welcome to transformational thinking, and transformational living, as we shape and reshape this generation and generations to come.

Final Thoughts

44

Humans are an indestructible Energy

Humans Are an Indestructible Energy

Humans are not just physical entities bound by flesh and bones; we are vibrant beings of energy. This energy is not just the life force that keeps our hearts beating but also the mental, emotional, and spiritual dynamism that defines our existence. Recognising ourselves as indestructible energy can profoundly transform our perspective on life, challenges, and our limitless potential.

Understanding Human Energy
At the most fundamental level, human beings are made of cells, which are composed of molecules, atoms, and subatomic particles; all of which are forms of energy. This concept aligns with the principles of quantum physics, which state that everything in the universe is energy vibrating at different frequencies. Our thoughts, emotions, and even physical states are forms of energy.

Illustration: Consider the human body as a complex electrical system. Just as electricity powers a machine, our body's energy flows through various channels, commonly referred to as chakras in Eastern philosophy, or meridians in Chinese medicine. These energy centres and pathways are crucial for maintaining physical health, emotional balance, and mental clarity.

Harnessing Mental and Emotional Energy
Our thoughts and emotions significantly impact our energy levels. Positive thoughts and emotions elevate our energy, while negative ones can deplete it. Understanding and managing this can help us maintain high energy levels and foster resilience.

Example: Imagine a day when you wake up feeling positive and motivated. You likely find it easier to accomplish tasks, interact harmoniously with others, and maintain focus. Conversely, waking up with negative thoughts or feelings can make even the simplest tasks feel burdensome, leading to a cycle of low energy and productivity.

Practical Application

Mindfulness Meditation: Practice mindfulness meditation to become aware of your thoughts and emotions. This awareness helps in managing and transforming negative thoughts into positive energy.

Affirmations: Use positive affirmations to boost your mental energy. Repeating statements like "I am capable," "I am resilient," and "I attract positive energy" can reprogram your subconscious mind to support a more positive outlook.

Physical Energy and Vitality

Our physical health is intrinsically linked to our energy levels. Regular exercise, a balanced diet, and adequate rest are fundamental to maintaining high energy levels. Physical activity is a powerful way to enhance energy flow throughout the body.

Example: Engaging in activities like yoga, tai chi, or even a brisk walk can significantly improve energy circulation, reduce stress, and increase vitality.

Practical Application:
Exercise Routine: Incorporate a regular exercise routine into your daily life. Activities such as jogging, swimming, or strength training can boost your physical energy and improve your well-being.

Healthy Eating: Consume a balanced diet rich in fruits, vegetables, lean proteins, and whole grains. Avoid excessive sugar and processed foods, which can lead to energy crashes.

Spiritual Energy and Connection

Beyond the physical and mental realms, spiritual energy is a profound aspect of our being. This energy connects us to a higher purpose and the larger universe. Cultivating spiritual energy can provide a deep sense of interconnectedness.

Illustration: Think of spiritual energy as the root system of a tree. Just as roots anchor the tree and provide nourishment, our spiritual energy grounds us and sustains our well-being.

Practical Application

Meditation and Prayer: Engage in regular meditation or prayer to connect with your higher self or a higher power. This practice can enhance your spiritual energy and provide guidance and clarity.

Acts of Kindness: Perform acts of kindness and compassion. Helping others not only boosts their energy but also elevates your own, creating a positive cycle of energy exchange.

The Indestructible Nature of Human Energy
One of the most empowering realisations is that our energy is indestructible. According to the law of conservation of energy, energy cannot be created or destroyed; it can only be transformed from one form to another. This principle applies to human energy as well. Our physical form may change, but the energy that constitutes our essence remains for all eternity.

Example: Consider the legacy of influential figures like Nikola Tesla, Martin Luther King Jr., or Marie Curie, who died long ago, but the energy of their thoughts, actions, and contributions continues to inspire and impact the world to this day.

Embracing Our Indestructible Energy

When faced with challenges, view them as opportunities to transform negative energy into positive outcomes. This mindset shift can lead to personal growth and resilience. Understanding and embracing the concept of indestructible energy empowers us to live with greater purpose and resilience. It encourages us to cultivate positive thoughts, maintain our physical health, nurture our spiritual connection, and create lasting impacts through our actions. As we conclude this book, "Transformational Thinking: Harnessing the Power of the Mind," remember that your journey is one of continuous transformation. Also remember that recognising and harnessing your indestructible energy will aid you navigating life's challenges with grace, achieve your goals, and contribute positively to the world. Embrace your limitless potential, and let your energy shine brightly, creating ripples of positive change far beyond your immediate reach. You can live a life that leaves an indelible mark on your generations and many generations beyond your earthly days. May your legacy outlive you.

45

About the Author

Dr David Kaluba stands as an epitome of empowerment in the realms of business and life coaching, renowned for his transformative methodologies that transcend boundaries. Author of several successful books and armed with a Ph.D. in Business Management among other accolades, from prestigious institutions like Kings College University of London, University of Southampton, Oxford University, and Harvard University, Dr Kaluba merges academic excellence with practical wisdom to propel individuals and organisations towards unprecedented success. His dynamic coaching style encompasses strategic goal setting, emotional intelligence, and mindfulness techniques, serving as catalysts for unlocking latent potential and fostering sustainable growth. Beyond his academic accolades, his diverse expertise spans across various domains, ranging from biomedical science to project management, banking and financial analysis.

As a certified transformational coach and NLP life and business coach, he navigates the intricacies of human behaviour and organisational dynamics with finesse, guiding his clients towards transformative breakthroughs. Additionally, his role as a mental health practitioner underscores his commitment to holistic well-being, recognising the inseparable link between personal fulfilment and professional achievement. At the helm of the DK Global Group and several charitable initiatives, Dr Kaluba exemplifies a steadfast dedication to societal betterment. Through platforms like the 'Winning in Life' podcast and his renowned 'Transformational Thinking' seminars, he shares invaluable insights and practical strategies for navigating life's complexities and unlocking boundless potential. His influence extends beyond mere coaching; he is a pillar of inspiration, igniting the flames of ambition and resilience in all who meet him.

His commitment to service extends to advisory roles on government boards, a testament to his unwavering dedication to community and humanity. He sees each opportunity to contribute to societal advancement as a privilege, leveraging his expertise and passion to foster positive change on a global scale. One of his greatest strengths lies in his ability to tailor his approach to meet the specific needs of each individual or organisation he works with. Whether he's guiding a Fortune 500 CEO through a period of transition or coaching a budding entrepreneur on goal-setting strategies, Dr Kaluba's commitment to excellence is unwavering. Beyond his professional achievements, he is known for his unwavering integrity, compassion, authenticity, infectious joy and love for people.

He approaches his work with humility and empathy, creating a safe and supportive environment for growth and self-discovery. His clients often describe him as a mentor, confidante, and change catalyst. His impact extends far beyond the boardroom or seminar hall. Through his philanthropic endeavours and community outreach initiatives, he is dedicated to making a difference in the lives of others through organisations such as, DK Global

Foundation, David Kaluba Foundation and Grace Church Global. His commitment to service is an integral part of who he is. With Dr Kaluba as your guide, the possibilities are limitless, and the future is bright. Get ready and prepare to be immersed in a world of possibility, where limitations dissolve, and aspirations soar. Through his guidance, you'll unearth the keys to unlocking your fullest potential, propelling you towards unparalleled success and satisfaction in both your business and personal life.

46

Epilogue

As we reach the end of *Transformational Thinking*, it's important to reflect on the journey we've undertaken together. This book has been a guide to not only understanding the complexities of personal growth but also to actively engaging in the transformative processes that lead to lasting change. The insights and strategies shared within these pages are designed to empower you, to help you harness your inner potential, and to inspire you to create a life that aligns with your deepest values and aspirations. Throughout our exploration, we've looked into the profound impact of mindset, the power of positive habits, and the importance of embracing progress over perfection. We've also examined how to construct empowering beliefs, the significance of finding meaning and purpose, and the critical role of aligning daily routines with your goals. Each chapter has aimed to provide you with practical tools and actionable steps, grounded in the principles of transformational thinking. The book has been written with the same clarity and understanding that I would normally use when presenting any subject in person.

But as with any journey, the real work begins once the book is closed. Transformation is not a destination but an ongoing process; it is a continuous evolution of self-discovery, growth, and renewal. The principles and practices outlined here are not mere concepts to be read but are invitations to be lived. They call you to actively engage with your own life story, to challenge and reshape old patterns, and to embrace the infinite possibilities that lie ahead. Remember, the path to transformation is unique for everyone. There will be moments of triumph and setbacks, periods of clarity and confusion. Through it all, the key is to remain committed to your journey. Seek progress, not perfection, and allow yourself the grace to evolve at your own pace. Celebrate your victories, however small, and learn from the challenges you encounter along the way. With every challenge in life, come valuable lessons for growth.

In the pursuit of your goals and dreams, may you find not only success but also deep satisfaction and fulfilment. May you cultivate resilience and compassion, both for yourself and for others. And may you continue to grow, to learn, and to live in alignment with your truest self. As you close this book and embark on your own transformational journey, carry with you the knowledge that you have within you the power to shape your reality and to create a life of profound meaning and purpose. Embrace the journey with an open heart and a fearless spirit, knowing that every step you take brings you closer to the life you envision. Thank you for allowing me to be a part of your transformational journey. The adventure of personal growth is ongoing, and I wish you every success as you continue to explore and realise your potential. Here's to the transformative path ahead and to the extraordinary possibilities that await.

With my deepest gratitude,
Dr David Kaluba

Printed in Great Britain
by Amazon